KU-269-189

THE WILES LECTURES GIVEN AT THE QUEEN'S UNIVERSITY
OF BELFAST, 1988

Domination and Conquest

Domination and Conquest

The experience of Ireland, Scotland and Wales 1100–1300

R. R. DAVIES

Professor of History, University College of Wales, Aberystwyth

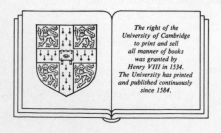

The right of the
University of Cambridge
to print and sell
all manner of books
was granted by
Henry VIII in 1534.
The University has printed
and published continuously
since 1584.

CAMBRIDGE UNIVERSITY PRESS

Cambridge

New York   Port Chester   Melbourne   Sydney

Published by the Press Syndicate of the University of Cambridge
The Pitt Building, Trumpington Street, Cambridge CB2 1RP
40 West 20th Street, New York, NY 10011, USA
10 Stamford Road, Oakleigh, Melbourne 3166, Australia

© Cambridge University Press 1990

First published 1990

Printed in Great Britain at the University Press, Cambridge

British Library cataloguing in publication data

Davies, R. R. (Robert Rees, *1938–*)
    Domination and conquest: the experience of Ireland,
    Scotland and Wales 1100–1300. (The Wiles lectures
    given at the Queen's University Belfast)
    1. Great Britain. 1154–1399
    I. Title
    941.03

Library of Congress cataloguing in publication data

Davies, R. R.
    Domination and conquest: the experience of Ireland,
    Scotland, and Wales, 1100–1300 / R. R. Davies.
       p.   cm. – (The Wiles lectures given at the Queen's University
    of Belfast)
    ISBN 0–521–38069–3
       1. Great Britain – History – Medieval period, 1066–1485.
    2. Ireland – History – To 1603.   3. Scotland – History – To 1603.
    4. Wales – History – To 1536.   I Title.   II Series Wiles lectures.
    DA175.D33   1990
    941–dc20   89–17385   CIP

ISBN 0 521 38069 3

CE

I Carys

Contents

Maps

Preface

This volume owes its origin to an invitation to deliver the Wiles Lectures at The Queen's University, Belfast for 1988. The terms of reference for the lectures are daunting. The lecturer is required 'to relate his researches to the general history of civilisation or to bring out the results of reflection on the wider implications of more detailed historical studies'. That is indeed a tall order for the modern academic historian, habituated as he is to the relative security of his own tiny patch of the historical garden and insured against criticism by a ring fence of scholarly footnotes. Nevertheless the invitation is not without its appeal. It incites the historian to choose a theme of general interest and gives him licence to trail his coat publicly on issues which academic prudence and coyness might normally have persuaded him to keep within the domain of his private thoughts.

It was in this spirit that I chose 'Domination and conquest' as the theme of my lectures. How one society comes to dominate, exploit and conquer another and how a subject people responds and adapts to the experience of domination are themes of perennial interest in the study of the past, as indeed of the present. I have chosen to consider them through a study of the Anglo-Norman and English domination of the British Isles in the twelfth and thirteenth centuries; but I hope that the issues I have raised have an interest and a resonance well beyond the geographical and chronological limits of this study. Those limits may appear narrow; even so, they have involved me in conducting plundering raids deep into Irish and, to a lesser extent, Scottish sources and historiography. I can only hope that the illumination that such a comparative approach may occasionally bring outweighs any misunderstandings and blunders on the part of a mere Welshman, *merus Wallicus*, trying to interpret the Scottish and Irish pasts.

No attempt has been made in this short volume to narrate the story of the Anglo-Norman and English penetration and domination of Ireland, Scotland and Wales in the period under consideration. There are ample such accounts (albeit too often fragmented by the constraints of national historiography), and I have leaned heavily on them. Rather what I have been concerned to try to analyse are the perceptions of relationships and the strategies of domination

ix

which underpin the narrative accounts, and the ways in which those perceptions and strategies changed over time. It is at this level, so it seems to me, that a comparative approach, taking the whole of the British Isles within its purview, may be particularly rewarding.

But comparisons may also bring their own distortions. In particular, I have been aware – and some of my audience at Belfast raised the level of my awareness uncomfortably higher – that it may be misleading to juxtapose Scotland on the one hand with Wales and Ireland on the other in an analysis of these two centuries. Scotland was a separate, unitary kingdom whose status was recognized by the kings of England and the rulers of the continent; its institutional and political development in the twelfth and thirteenth centuries placed it in a league altogether different from that of the small native polities of Wales and Ireland; its kings were deeply influenced by French and Anglo-Norman habits and moved easily in the social circles of the monarchs and aristocrats of England and northern Europe; and the Anglo-Norman penetration of the country took a very different form, and with diametrically different results, from that it assumed in Ireland and Wales. None of that can be gainsaid, nor should it be overlooked at any stage in the argument of this book. Yet the Scottish experience, so it seems to me, does illuminate the story of Anglo-Norman expansion in, and English domination of, the British Isles in a significant fashion, by way both of comparison and contrast with the experience of Wales and Ireland. That is why I have occasionally, and no doubt very inadequately, drawn upon it in the course of this book.

A few words may help to explain, if not to excuse, certain presentational aspects of this volume. Chapters 1, 2, 3 and 6 contain the text of the Wiles Lectures much as they were delivered in Belfast; their style reflects, no doubt, their declamatory origin. Chapters 4 and 5, dealing with issues which could not be squeezed into the lectures themselves, but were too important to be overlooked, may well convey the more austere atmosphere of the private study late at night. I hope the disjunction between the two genres is not too unsettling. I was taken to task at Belfast for using the terms 'Anglo-Norman' (and its variants 'Anglo-French' or 'Cambro-Norman' or plain 'Norman') and 'English' in an inconsistent and misleading fashion. I have tried to reduce the inconsistency by referring, broadly speaking, to 'Normans' and 'Anglo-Normans' before *c.* 1170–1200, to 'English' thereafter. I take comfort and historical reassurance in the fact that the ambiguity was a contemporary one: the invasion of Ireland in 1169–70 was known both as a Norman (or French) invasion *and* as an English conquest, while Welsh sources likewise hesitated between the terms 'French' (Norman) and 'English' to describe the alien settlers and conquerors of Wales. In the spelling of Irish personal names I have – quite possibly to the initial discomfiture of English readers – employed the vernacular forms used in A. Cosgrove, ed., *A New History of Ireland*, volume II: *Medieval Ireland 1169–1534* (Oxford, 1987). A Welsh-speaking Welshman (albeit one whose first name is Rees!) could hardly do otherwise.

This is a small volume, but its Preface must end with a large vote of thanks – to Mrs Janet Boyd whose munificence created the Wiles Trust and who graced the lectures with her presence; to the Trustees for extending to me the honour to deliver the lectures; to Professor Lewis Warren and his colleagues at Queen's who made my stay there such a memorably happy and hospitable one; to the companionable band of scholars from universities in England, Scotland, Wales, Ireland and Denmark who were invited by the Wiles Trust to attend the lectures and were as shrewd and courteous a group of critics as any lecturer could have; to Dr Robin Frame who as well as enduring the lectures did me the great service of reading the volume in typescript and from whose acute comments I should have benefited even more than I have done; and to Mrs Margaret White and Miss Linda James for coping with various redactions of the volume over a long period. To all, my thanks.

May 1989   R.R.D.

Abbreviations

The following abbreviations are used throughout in the footnotes:

Anc. Corr. conc. Wales	*Calendar of Ancient Correspondence concerning Wales*, ed. J. G. Edwards (Cardiff, 1935).
Anderson, *Scottish Annals*	*Scottish Annals from English Chroniclers A.D. 500 to 1286*, ed. A. O. Anderson (London, 1908).
Anderson, *Early Sources of Scottish History*	*Early Sources of Scottish History A.D. 500 to 1286*, ed. A. O. Anderson, 2 vols. (Edinburgh, 1922).
Barrow, *Anglo-Norman Era*	G. W. S. Barrow, *The Anglo-Norman Era in Scottish History* (Oxford, 1980).
Barrow, *Bruce*	G. W. Barrow, *Robert Bruce and the Community of the Realm of Scotland*, 3rd edn (Edinburgh, 1988).
Barrow, *Kingship and Unity*	G. W. S. Barrow, *Kingship and Unity. Scotland 1000–1306* (London, 1981).
Brut	*Brut y Tywysogyon or The Chronicle of the Princes. Peniarth Ms. 20 version*, ed. and trans. Thomas Jones (Cardiff, 1952).
Brut (R. B. H.)	*Brut y Tywysogyon or The Chronicle of the Princes. Red Book of Hergest Version*, ed. and trans. Thomas Jones (Cardiff, 1955).
CDI	*Calendar of Documents relating to Ireland 1171–1307*, ed. H. S. Sweetman, 5 vols. (London, 1875–86).
Davies, *Conquest*	R. R. Davies, *Conquest, Coexistence and Change: Wales 1063–1415* (Oxford, 1987).
Descr. Kambrie	Giraldus Cambrensis, *Descriptio Kambrie*, in *Opera*, ed. J. S. Brewer *et al.* Rolls Series (8 vols., London, 1861–91), vol. VI.
Duncan, *Scotland*	A. A. M. Duncan, *Scotland: The Making of the Kingdom* (Edinburgh, 1975).
Expugnatio	Giraldus Cambrensis, *Expugnatio Hibernica: The Conquest of Ireland*, ed. A. B. Scott and F. X. Martin (Dublin, 1978). Also available in Giraldus Cambren-

	sis, *Opera*, ed. J. S. Brewer *et al.* Rolls Series (8 vols., London 1861–91), vol. v.
Itin. Kambrie	Giraldus Cambrensis, *Itinerarium Kambrie*, in *Opera*, ed. J. S. Brewer *et al.* Rolls Series (8 vols., London, 1861–91), vol. vi.
Litt. Wallie	*Littere Wallie preserved in Liber A in the Public Record Office*, ed. J. G. Edwards (Cardiff, 1940).
NHI, vol. ii	*A New History of Ireland*, vol. ii. *Medieval Ireland 1169–1534*, ed. A. Cosgrove (Oxford, 1987).
Otway-Ruthven, *Ireland*	A. J. Otway-Ruthven, *A History of Medieval Ireland*, 2nd edn (London, 1980).
Song	*The Song of Dermot and the Earl*, ed. G. H. Orpen (Oxford, 1892).

Map 1 Ireland: chief places mentioned in the text

MORAY

ARGYLL

CLYDESDALE

BUTE

CUNNINGHAM

KINTYRE

AYRSHIRE

ANNANDALE

GALLOWAY

SOLWAY FIRTH

Abernethy •
Dunfermline •

LOTHIAN
LAUDERDALE
TWEEDDALE

Selkirk •   Kelso •

Berwick •
Norham •

Alnwick •

Carlisle •

Newcastle
upon Tyne •

N

0   20   40 miles

0   20   40   60 km

Map 2 Scotland: chief places mentioned in the text

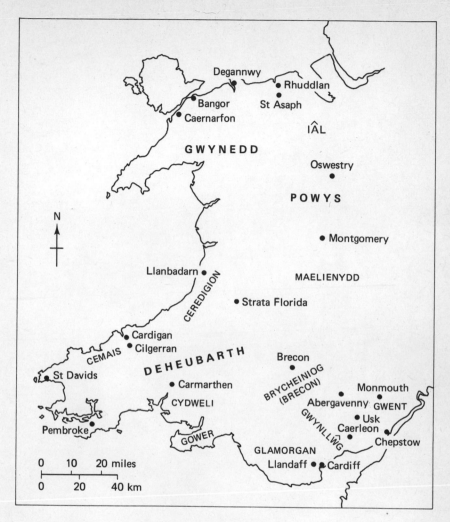

Map 3 Wales: chief places mentioned in the text

I

Patterns of domination

Historians, so we have been assured, are quiet men.[1] Nevertheless they have a soft spot for conquest, the more sudden, clear-cut and overwhelming the better. The reasons are not far to seek. Conquests simplify the historian's life and help him to tame an intractable past. In particular they provide him with a ready-made chronology, a series of memorable dates which serve to divide the past into neat, manageable segments. Where would the English historian be without his 1066, the Irish historian without 1169 or his Welsh colleague without 1282? The Scots may not find it so easy to latch on to a single date, but for them likewise the struggle against the English attempt to subdue Scotland and battles such as Stirling Bridge (1297) and Bannockburn (1314) serve as important chronological markers in recounting the country's history.

Such a conquest-dominated chronology is not merely a tool of convenience devised by and for historians; more often than not it was a view of the world shared by contemporaries and vigorously promoted by the conquerors. Triumphs were celebrated and actively recalled, if only as a firm reminder of who were the winners and who the losers. So it was that Henry II was memorialized as 'conqueror' and 'victor of Ireland' and Edward I mourned as 'the conqueror of lands and flower of chivalry'; so likewise, English settlers in Wales in the mid-fourteenth century looked back wistfully to the days of 'the good king Edward the Conqueror'.[2] The past was divided to conform to this mood of triumphalism. Thus the Normans in England proclaimed both the finality of their conquest and the legitimacy of their regime by their references to 'the day that King Edward was alive and dead'; in Ireland the great divide was that between 'the time of the Irish' (*in tempore Hibernicorum*) on the one hand and 'the time of the conquest of the said land' on the other; while in Wales Edward I drew a neat and definitive line across the past by decreeing that 'the proclamation of our peace in Wales in our eleventh year' (1283)

---

[1] J. Campbell, E. John and P. Wormald, *The Anglo-Saxons* (Oxford, 1982), p. 54.
[2] J. T. Gilbert (ed.), *Chartularies of St Mary's Abbey, Dublin* (Rolls Series, 2 vols., London, 1884), vol. 1, p. 530; G. O. Sayles (ed.), *Documents on the Affairs of Ireland Before the King's Council*, Irish Manuscript Commission (Dublin, 1979), p. 64; Barrow, *Bruce*, p. 60; *Anc. Corr. conc. Wales*, p. 234.

should be the *terminus a quo* for legal actions and thereby of legal memory.[3] The conqueror had imposed his own chronology, more specifically the chronology of his victory, on the collective and official memory of the past. Historians on the whole, for reasons of convenience and simplicity, have gone along with that chronology of victory in their division and interpretation of the past.

They have also often subscribed, wittingly or otherwise, to the conqueror's view of the significance of his victory, notably to the belief that it inaugurated a period of profound change – not only in military supremacy but also in a whole host of other matters, social, economic, cultural and ecclesiastical. The temptation to cast conquest in this rôle of an explanatory *deus ex machina* is all the greater since conquest is often accompanied – as in Ireland from 1169 or Wales from 1282 – by a dramatic change in the character of the records available to the historian. It is through the documentation of the conqueror that the conquest itself has largely to be studied and it is mainly on *his* terms, therefore, that the consequences of his conquest have been viewed. It is, perhaps, inevitable that the military should have most of the good shots and that the military victors should have the best shots of all. It is, nevertheless, remarkable how far in our history books we have aligned our explanations of social, economic and cultural change to a chronology of military victory and political dominance; nowhere more so than in the history of conquered societies such as Ireland and Wales. After all, the ultimate compliment to the significance of a military conquest is to assume that it did transform the character of the conquered society. Historians have been too ready, perhaps, to pay that compliment.

Conquests have yet one further seductive appeal to the historian. They can be readily assimilated to the national framework within which we overwhelmingly package our histories – English, Irish, Scottish, Welsh and so forth. In the unfolding of such national sagas, from whatever viewpoint we write them, conquests, attempted or successful, have pride of place; they are crucial milestones in the national memory and, often, in forging national identity. There is indeed ample contemporary confirmation of the way that memories of conquest have dominated the collective national psyche. The historical mythologies of both Ireland and Wales show that clearly enough. In Ireland the classic historical tradition was encapsulated in two works which dwelt on the themes of invasion, conquest and resistance – 'The Book of Invasions' (Leabhar Gabhála) and the later 'War of the Irish against the Foreigners' (Cogadh Gaedhel re Gallaibh). Within such a tradition it was natural enough

---

3 For England see esp. G. Garnett, 'Coronation and Propaganda: some Implications of the Norman claim to the Throne of England in 1066', *Transactions of the Royal Historical Society*, 5th ser., 36 (1986), pp. 91–116; for Ireland, *Chart. St Mary's Dublin*, vol. 1, p. 387; *Song*, p. 314; *Documents on the Affairs of Ireland*, p. 35; *Close Rolls of the reign of Henry III* (14 vols. London, 1902–38), 1254–6, p. 413; for Wales, *Statues of the Realm* (11 vols. London, 1810–28), vol. 1, pp. 55–70.

to add the Anglo-Normans as the latest in a list of 'foreign tyrants'.[4] In Wales, similarly, native historical learning spoke bitterly of the Three Oppressions (Gormesoedd) of the Island of Britain.[5] In other words in both countries memories and mythologies of the past were structured very considerably in terms of conquests and invasions. It was easy to assimilate the latest invaders, the Anglo–Normans, into such a pattern of conquests and oppressions.

Yet we must be on our guard. The Anglo-Normans did not set out self-consciously on a conquest of 'Wales' or 'Ireland' as such, or plot the take-over of the kingdom of Scotland; they were not informed by national ambitions or national animus; few of them could have guessed at, or cared about, what they might – or might not – achieve; as often as not they came by invitation and participated with gusto in the free-for-all which we call Welsh or Irish politics; at first at least they were not seen as different from, or more menacing than, earlier foreign invaders or allies; and they for their part adjusted rapidly to their new habitat and brought their subjects – be they French, English, Flemings, Irish, Welsh or Scots – within their ample, non-discriminating, ecumenical embrace.[6] In short their enterprises were not national conquests in intention, scale or character. That they eventually came to be seen as such is largely to be explained by changing ambitions and perceptions, especially from the early-thirteenth century onwards, and by the national orientation and inescapable hindsight of modern historiographical interpretation.

We might, therefore, be well advised to approach the concept of conquest circumspectly. Equally, we should not allow the military the sole prerogative of telling it as it was. The reality and brutality of conquest, of course, are not in doubt; but conquest in the sense of a military act is only one of the routes to the domination of one society by another and not necessarily the most attractive, rewarding or important of such routes. As a strictly military enterprise a conquest can no doubt be described exclusively on its own terms; but as a part of a process of domination it needs surely to be placed in a wider context. It is the cursory investigation of that wider context – in terms of the texture of relationships and the balances of power but also in terms of perceptions of dependence and the establishment of norms of superiority – which is the theme of this first chapter.

Where better to start than with the ideology of the very rulers and aristocracies – the kings and barons of Norman and Angevin England – who

[4] See, for example, the contemporary poem quoted by K. Simms, 'The Battle of Dysert O'Dea', *Dal gCais* 5 (1979), 59; 'From the time Brian (Boroihme) was slain, foreigners did not inhabit Ireland until the present day, with the arrival of the Earl (Strongbow)'.

[5] R. Bromwich (ed.), *Trioedd Ynys Prydein. The Welsh Triads*, 2nd edn (Cardiff, 1978), pp. 84–7.

[6] For writs with multiple address clauses see, for example, T. Phillips (ed.), *Cartularium Prioratus St Johannis Baptiste de Carmarthen* (Cheltenham, 1865), no. 33; J. T. Gilbert (ed.), *Register of the Abbey of St Thomas, Dublin*, Rolls Series (London, 1869), pp. 214–15, 226–7.

had the will and the means to decide what forms their domination might take. They were, by and large, men of instinct and action, not men of contemplation and rationalization. However, in so far as we can hope to penetrate their thought-world, we can rest assured that they would have no qualms about the prospect or propriety of domination. It was their business. Furthermore, contemporary historical mythologies invited them to think big, in terms of Britain, *Britannia*, or even indeed of the British Isles *tout court*. The Welsh had surrendered even before the struggle began: William the Conqueror's obit in the native Welsh chronicle already recognized him as 'prince of the Normans and king of the Saxons and Britons and the Scots', while his son, Henry I, was saluted as 'King of England and Wales' and, for good measure in one redaction, 'of all the island besides'. Domination of the British Isles had been handed to them on a plate. As for Ireland, few Anglo-Normans who gave the matter any thought would have dissented from Gerald of Wales' view that Ireland 'is the lawful possession of the kings of Britain'; they would have backed up their opinion by recalling how King Arthur had sailed to Ireland and conquered the whole of it and how Ireland's king had thereafter obediently turned up at Arthur's court at Caerleon.[8] The need to expound the historical basis of English supremacy over Scotland came rather later; but when Edward I was called upon to explain the 'right and dominion that belong to us in the realm of Scotland' he did so eventually (in 1301, but not in 1291) by appealing to his superior right as the descendant of Locrine, the eldest son of Brutus of Troy, the first king of all Britain after the expulsion of the giants.[9] The historical mythology of English overlordship of the British Isles, therefore, had an almost immemorial resonance to it.

It was, furthermore, a mythology amply supported by a much more contemporary theory and practice of domination. The Wessex dynasty in the tenth century had proudly paraded its pan-British claims by arrogating such resounding titles as 'emperor', 'basileus' or 'king of the whole of Britain'. Aethelred the Unraed, for example, gave himself the grandiloquent title 'king of the English and governor of the other adjacent lands roundabout'.[10] The Norman kings steered clear of such inflated titles; but their archbishops did not – Lanfranc describing himself as primate of all Britain (*primas Britanniarum, totius Britanniae primas*) and Anselm's biographer claiming that Canterbury's jurisdiction extended to 'the whole of England, Scotland, Ireland and

---

7 *Brut*, pp. 18, 51; *Brut (RBH)*, pp. 112–13.

8 *Expugnatio*, pp. 252–3 (Bk 2, ch. 39); Gerald of Wales, *The History and Topography of Ireland*, ed. J. J. O'Meara (Harmondsworth, 1982), pp. 99–100; Geoffrey of Monmouth, *History of the Kings of Britain*, ed. L. Thorpe (Harmondsworth, 1966), pp. 101, 221–2, 227.

9 E. L. G. Stones (ed.), *Anglo-Scottish Relations 1174–1328. Some Selected Documents*, 2nd edn (Oxford, 1970), pp. 194–7.

10 E. John, *Orbis Britanniae and Other Essays* (Leicester, 1966), esp. pp. 48–63; D. Whitelock (ed.), *English Historical Documents c. 500–1042*. 2nd edn (London, 1979), p. 569 (no. 117); cf. pp. 575, 578 (no. 120: 'King of the English and governor of the whole orbit of Britain'); p. 590 (no. 127: 'governing the monarchy of all Albion').

the adjacent isles'.[11] Nor were such pretensions to domination idle fantasy. As far as Wales was concerned there is ample evidence of Welsh kings submitting themselves to the English, swearing oaths to be loyal and faithful underkings (even in their moments of success), attending the king's court, surrendering hostages and paying tribute – both before and after the Norman conquest. In Scotland, likewise, it could not be denied that Scottish kingship had been reduced, at least spasmodically, to client status *vis à vis* the stronger kingship of Wessex-England, again both before and after the Norman conquest. No such evidence could be produced in respect of Ireland, but the fact that the bishops of Dublin, Waterford and Limerick had gone to Canterbury to be consecrated might suggest that where ecclesiastical supremacy led, political domination might sooner or later follow.[12] In short, the historical mythology and the political ideology and practice of English domination of the British Isles were, in many respects, already well in place before the process of the so-called Anglo-Norman conquest of Britain began.

So also were many of the strategies of domination. Domination is often most successfully asserted where it is unplanned and unconscious, where it arises (as it were) out of the natural weft of political relationships. So it often was in medieval Britain. Political exiles and refugees fled from England to Wales, Ireland and Scotland; from Wales to Ireland and England; and no doubt likewise from Scotland and Ireland to wherever was convenient. Troops were hired, alliances forged, and marriages arranged. So were ties of friendship, mutual benefit and dependence formed which might in other circumstances blossom into clientship and domination. Thus when Diarmait mac Maél na mBó, king of Leinster 1047–72, gave asylum to the sons of Harold Godwinson after 1066 and, quite possibly, employed Norman mercenaries in his service, such acts could well have initiated a relationship of dependence between Leinster and England a century before the 'conquest' of 1169.[13] One could stumble into domination – or dependence – unexpectedly, almost against the odds. Thus when the mighty house of Montgomery, earls of Shrewsbury and Pembroke and lords of vast estates in England, Normandy and France, were down on their luck in 1101–2 they turned to the Welsh for succour and to the Irish for a marriage alliance, calculating, no doubt, that today's necessity might turn out to be tomorrow's opportunity and that the marriage bed is one of the easiest, cheapest and most comfortable routes to domination. The Montgomeries took the world as they found it, exploring it ruthlessly to their own ends, living for the moment, not knowing what good luck or (as it turned

[11] J. A. Watt, *The Church and the Two Nations in Medieval Ireland* (Cambridge, 1970), pp. 217–18.
[12] For Wales see Wendy Davies, *Wales in the Early Middle Ages* (Leicester, 1982), pp. 112–16; Davies, *Conquest*, pp. 27, 42; for Scotland, Duncan, *Scotland*, pp. 94–100, 119–30, 216–18; J. Le Patourel, *The Norman Empire* (Oxford, 1976), pp. 57–8, 67–73; for Ireland, Watt, *The Church and the Two Nations*, pp. 7–9, 217–25.
[13] *NHI*, vol. II p. 22.

out) disastrous misfortune might attend their ambitions. Domination might
be a contingent result of their ambitions; but so equally might be disaster.
Likewise when a king of Gwynedd or Deheubarth in Wales or of Ulaid
(Ulster) or Leinster in Ireland summoned help from the Vikings of Dublin,
the Norsemen of the Hebrides, the men of Argyll or the Anglo-Normans
they were not involved in some heinous act of national surrender. Nor were
they aware that they might be contributing to a process which historians,
with the benefit of hindsight, label a 'conquest'. They were simply pursuing
their current ambitions in conventional ways and with whatever means there
were to hand. No more and no less. In this world submission and domination were rarely part of some grand strategy; rather were they the incidental and often very short-lived by-products of the needs of the political or
military moment.

Furthermore domination was often in effect secured, as in all periods, by
tactics in which the kid glove rather than the mailed fist was to the fore.
Native princes might be won over by gifts, for, as the Welsh chronicler
observed, 'it was the custom of the French to deceive men with promises';[14]
social visits were encouraged; attention was lavished and flattery ladled in
ample measure. By such means were men gradually attracted into the social
orbit of the Normans and Angevins, to learn their manners and to ape their
ways. We need not interpret all such social events cynically or suspiciously.
Yet they do assuredly have their significance in the strategy of domination.
The kings and nobles of England were demonstrating their social superiority
and the magnetism of their courts and their *mores*. The kings of Scotland
and the princes of Wales for their part were, in the contemporary Irish
phrase for submission, entering the king of England's house, literally so.
Social submission was often the acceptable face of political deference.

Domination was being achieved without conquest; the transparent superiority of power was enough to effect it. Thus Scotland's history between 1097
and 1135 showed clearly that effective political tutelage could be achieved
without military confrontation, let alone conquest. King Edgar (1097–1107)
indeed went so far as to acknowledge in a charter that he held his kingdom
'by gift of King William (Rufus)' as well as 'by paternal inheritance'.[15] He
further showed his deference towards his English patron by bearing the cere-
monial sword at Rufus' crown-wearing in 1099. Likewise, though admittedly
under very different circumstances, Scotland between 1174 and 1189 lay once
more, in the words of a contemporary chronicle, 'under the heavy yoke of
domination and servitude' without an English army having crossed the border.[16] As for Wales, Gerald was quite firm in his opinion that it 'is a portion

[14] *Brut*, p. 39.
[15] A. A. M. Duncan, 'The Earliest Scottish Charters', *Scottish Historical Review*, 37 (1958),
103–35.
[16] Chronicle of Melrose in Anderson, *Sources*, vol. II p. 323.

of the kingdom of England, not a kingdom in itself'.[17] The Welsh may have cared to believe otherwise; but Henry I and Henry II had little difficulty in showing that any qualified measure of independence that the Welsh principalities enjoyed was entirely dependent on the sufferance and goodwill of the king of England. The occasional royal expedition – in 1114, 1121, 1157–8 and 1165 – served to remind the Welsh of that grim reality. They were not campaigns of conquest nor were they followed by the installation of garrisons in Wales; but they were demonstrations of domination and brisk reminders to the Welsh of what power could be brought to bear against them. Most tellingly of all, domination could even operate at a distance and across the sea. In a deservedly famous passage William of Malmesbury remarked that Muirchertach O Briain (Murtough O'Brien), king of Munster 1086–1119, and his successors were so terrified of Henry I of England that 'they would write nothing but what would please him and do nothing but what he commanded'.[18] With however large a pinch of salt we take the comment, it admirably expresses how contemporaries recognized the symptoms of political dependence, of satellite status short, as it were, of sending in the tanks.

William had a ready explanation for Ireland's political submissiveness, namely its commercial dependence on England. 'For what would Ireland be worth', he asked rhetorically, 'if goods were not brought to her from England?' Gerald of Wales echoed precisely the same view later when he remarked that 'Ireland cannot survive without the goods and trade which come to it from Britain'.[19] Both claims are doubtless exaggerated; but they assuredly have their point and significance. They help to direct our attention away from the narrowly political and military aspects of domination to the broader context of dependence. Economic ties were a major aspect of that dependence. The commercial links between eastern and southern Ireland and England, notably through Bristol and Chester, were doubtless far more extensive than the exiguous literary evidence would suggest.[20] It is significant that it was in the house of a rich Bristol merchant, Robert fitz Harding, that Diarmait Mac Murchada (Dermot MacMurrough), king of Leinster 1126–71, and his family sought refuge in 1166. It is equally indicative of the link between commercial power and political control that one of Henry II's first policy decisions on his expedition to Ireland in 1171–2 was to reserve the key trading towns of Dublin, Waterford, Cork and Limerick for the English crown. Commercial relationships, as so often, were the prelude to political ties.

[17] H. E. Butler (ed.), *The Autobiography of Giraldus Cambrensis* (London, 1937), p. 183.
[18] William of Malmesbury, *De Gestis Regum Anglorum libri quinque*, ed. W. Stubbs, Rolls Series (2 vols., London, 1887–9), vol. II, pp. 484–5.
[19] *Expugnatio*, p. 253 (Bk 2, ch. 39).
[20] P. F. Wallace, 'Anglo-Norman Dublin: Continuity and Change', *Irish Antiquity. Essays and Studies Presented to M. J. O'Kelly* (Cork, 1981), pp. 247–67; M. Richter, 'The European Dimension of Irish History in the Eleventh and Twelfth Centuries', *Peritia*, 4 (1985), pp. 328–45.

Much the same was true of Wales. Shrewd contemporaries were well aware of that and were not in doubt about the consequences. 'Wales is incapable of supplying its inhabitants with food without imports from the adjacent counties of England', remarked William of Newburgh in the later twelfth century. 'And since it cannot command this without the liberality or express permission of the king of England, it is necessarily subject to his power.' The point could not have been put more trenchantly, and was echoed by Gerald of Wales.[21] For both authors commercial dependence opened the door to political control. William and Gerald may have been guilty of oversimplification in their characterization of the economic order in Wales; they also underestimated the political resilience of Wales and overstated its commercial dependence on England. Nevertheless their comments were surely perceptive; historians should have paid more heed to them. Wales in the eleventh and twelfth centuries was by north-western European standards an under-developed country, especially in terms of markets, towns, trade and the use of coin. It was ripe for exploitation. And exploited it was, especially for its slaves, timber, hides, furs, flocks and herds. During the twelfth and thirteenth centuries an army of foreign merchants, townsmen and settlers bound Wales, more especially southern lowland Wales, to an increasingly England-oriented economy and trade network. Once that happened, political domination would follow, sooner or later. However remarkable the resurgence and resilience of Welsh native power may have been in these centuries, it was fatally stunted by its failure to recover the economically rich and commercially developed lowlands of south-east and south-west Wales, now securely under Anglo-Norman control.

Scotland's story was in many respects different; but there likewise the English model proved a powerful, if by no means the only, incentive to a remarkable economic transformation. Scotland had probably no burghs and no coinage of its own at the outset of the twelfth century; a hundred years later forty or so boroughs flourished and a standard royal coinage, minted at many of the major boroughs, circulated widely in the country. This remarkable transformation had been effected under the aegis of the Scottish kings: most of the early burghs were founded by them, on land belonging to them, and enjoyed marketing and other monopolies conferred by them. But equally striking is Anglo-Norman inspiration, imitation and impetus in the history of this urban revolution. Contemporaries and historians are agreed that the population of these early Scottish towns came overwhelmingly from England, especially eastern England, and to a lesser extent northern France, Flanders and the Rhineland; 'the language of business was English'; the customs of the English royal borough of Newcastle upon Tyne became the exemplar of the

---

[21] William of Newburgh, 'Historia Rerum Anglicarum', *Chronicles of the Reigns of Stephen, Henry II and Richard I*, ed. R. Howlett, Rolls Series (4 vols., London 1884–9), vol. I, p. 107; *Descr. Kambrie*, p. 218 (Bk 2, ch. 8).

Scottish 'Laws of the Four Burghs'; Scottish coinage closely resembled that of the Norman and Angevin ruler of England in style and silver content; while Scottish inter-regional trade 'was an extension of the interregional trade of England and depended greatly upon movements in London commercial circles'.[22]

What this amounts to claiming, in a tentative fashion, is that English economic domination was penetrating, at varying pace, to different parts of the British Isles, partly through the control of a good deal of foreign trade, partly in providing items of commerce (both raw materials and finished products) without which the economies of these districts could not survive or flourish, and partly in providing the exemplars, expertise, manpower and ample stocks of coins for forging new economic relationships. Commercial links and economic penetration need not lead to, or be preceded by, political domination. But the link is often close. William of Newburgh had recognized as much. So had Gerald of Wales: when he drew up his blueprint for the conquest of Wales one of his recommendations was the establishment of an embargo on the import into Wales of iron, cloth, salt and corn.[23] Kings of thirteenth-century England certainly tried to impose such economic blockades, whether against Scotland in 1244 or Wales in 1277, while their lieutenants likewise soon recognized that economic strangleholds can quickly lead to political surrender. Domination can take more than one form.

There was more, however, to such commercial power than its political potential; it was but one expression of what the Anglo-Normans regarded as their self-evident economic superiority. William of Malmesbury may again serve as their spokesman: 'Her soil', he remarked of Ireland, 'is so poor and the tillers of her soil so ignorant that it can only sustain a rustic and beggarly crowd of Irishmen outside the cities. But Englishmen and Frenchmen, having a more civilized way of life, dwell in cities and are familiar with trade and commerce.'[24] At one level it matters little whether the comment is accurate or not; it is the perception and assumptions behind it which are instructive. Domination is often based on perceptions of relative status, be it of political power, economic wealth or social and cultural development. William's views were quite clear and were widely shared by his fellow countrymen: the Irish (and the same could certainly have been said of the Welsh) were economically and technologically backward, whereas he belonged to a people which was commercially superior and urbanized and thereby civilized and urbane. Nor can his picture be gainsaid. Whatever allowances we may care to make for the overdrawn and oversimplified characterization of the economic and social life

---

[22] See in general Duncan, *Scotland*, chaps. 18–19 and Barrow, *Kingship and Unity*, ch. 5. The quotations are from A. A. M. Duncan, *The Nation of Scots and the Declaration of Arbroath*, Historical Association (London, 1970), p. 8 and Duncan, *Scotland*, p. 518.

[23] *Descr. Kambrie*, pp. 218–19 (Bk 2, ch. 8). Cf. the comment of the Dunstable annalist, H. R. Luard (ed.), *Annales Monastici*, Rolls Series (5 vols., London, 1864–9), vol. III, p. 165.

[24] *De Gestis Regum*, vol. II, p. 485.

of pre-Norman Ireland, Scotland and Wales in the writings of Anglo-Norman commentators,[25] it is difficult to deny that the coming of the Anglo-Normans represented the triumph of a vibrant, confident, aggressive economic mentality which had come to dominate north-western Europe from the second half of the eleventh century. In terms of the exploitation of resources, the marketing of produce, and availability of money as a unit of exchange, the centrality of the town in the exchange and distribution of surpluses and the ability to sustain a (by contemporary standards) large and socially-differentiated population the Anglo-Normans surely belonged to a new world. And they knew it.

Their memorials are not merely or even mainly mottes, ringworks and castles; they are equally and ultimately more importantly, towns, manors, villages, fields, mills, limekilns, and bridges. One example may serve to demonstrate how they brought their economic entrepreneurship to bear in newly conquered lands. By 1086 – in other words within a very few years of their arrival in north Wales – they had founded (or refounded) a borough at Rhuddlan on the Clwyd estuary, enclosed it with earthworks which embraced an area of thirty-five acres, established a mint there, built mills, collected tolls and exploited the fisheries of the area and its iron deposits. There is no need to claim that in Rhuddlan or elsewhere the Anglo-Normans built *de novo*; but the way they chose their sites in Wales and later in Ireland, quickly organized the lineaments of manorial organization and demesne farming, seized on the pastoral and arable resources of their newly conquered lordships, founded boroughs, built mills and recruited settlers speaks volumes of their entrepreneurial attitude.[26] It was an attitude which they shared with men such as the counts of Champagne and Flanders who likewise reclaimed lands, invited settlers to occupy them, founded towns and encouraged trade. Avarice, *cupiditas*, was the besetting sin of these men; it was a sin which Gerald of Wales quickly recognized in the Anglo-Normans (whereas the Welsh clung to old fashioned habits such as liberty, *libertas*).[27]

It was Gerald again who best captured the two essential qualities of these men – their tough militarism and their quick eye for profit – in his memorable description of the Flemings of his native Pembroke. They were, he said, 'a strong and hardy people, deeply imbued with hostility towards the Welsh through continuous battle with them; but a people who spared no labour and feared no danger by sea or by land in their search for profit (*lucrum*); a people

[25] In Ireland in particular allowance needs to be made for commercial and economic development in the century and more before 1170, especially in southern and eastern Ireland. Dr Robin Frame reminded me of this important qualification.
[26] Davies, *Conquest*, pp. 97–100, 158–62; *NHI*, vol. II, pp. 157, 165–7, 212–14, 221–5, 459–61, 467–70, 480–1; G. Cunningham, *The Anglo-Norman Advance into the South-West Midlands of Ireland 1185–1221* (Roscrea, 1987), pp. xvii–xxv.
[27] *Descr. Kambrie*, p. 226 (Bk 2, ch. 10): 'Praesertim etiam cum Angli pro cupiditate certent, Kambri pro libertate'. For contemporary condemnations of avarice as a 'dominant vice' of the period, see A. Murray, *Reason and Society in the Middle Ages* (Oxford, 1978), ch. 3.

as well fitted to follow the plough as to wield the sword'.[28] The domination of the British Isles was won by such men, by their economic enterprise as much as by their physical prowess; their domination was entrepreneurial as much as it was military. Indeed the Scottish experience would suggest that the former could triumph where the latter had not been much called upon. There is no need, of course, to ascribe the economic changes of the twelfth and thirteenth centuries solely to the Anglo-Normans; but it is difficult not to believe that they did at least transform the tempo and scale of economic activity within the lowland peripheries of the British Isles which came, directly or indirectly, within their orbit – whether in Gower or Cydweli in Wales or in Knocktopher (co. Kilkenny) or in the coastal manors of the earldom of Ulster in Ireland.[29] Their entrepreneurship, their novel economic methods and technologies, and their conviction of their own economic superiority, were both an expression and a cause of the domination they came to enjoy.

That domination was also the domination of a new people. The Anglo-Norman penetration of Wales, Ireland and Scotland was not merely, or even mainly, an aristocratic affair; it was vitally underpinned by considerable popular migration. Military conquest has often been given priority in the history books, if only because military events appear to provide a firm story line and fixed chronological reference points; but in any rounded analysis of domination colonization should surely occupy an equally important place.

One group of colonists, the Flemings, has indeed received considerable attention from historians. They formed a vigorous and distinctive community in south-west Wales – mainly, but not exclusively, in southern Pembroke – after they were first introduced there by Henry I. They continued to speak their native tongue in the area until at least the late twelfth century; and more than a generation later could still be identified by the native Welsh annalist as a group separate both from the French and the English.[30] The Flemings may have contributed substantially to the colonization of Ireland in the late twelfth century; they were certainly occasionally identified as a separate group there. They seem to have settled extensively also in parts of northern England and it may be that it was from there that they migrated to those parts of Scotland, notably Clydesdale and Moray, where Flemish settlements seem to be particularly marked. In some cases, such as that of the de Quincy family, it is possible to trace a family from Flanders pursuing its fortune, accompanied by

---

[28] *Itin. Kambrie*, p. 83 (Bk 1, ch. 11).
[29] J. B. Smith in T. B. Pugh (ed.), *Glamorgan County History*, vol. ii (Cardiff, 1971), pp. 208–13; Davies, *Conquest*, pp. 96–9; C. A. Empey, 'Medieval Knocktopher: A Study in Manorial Settlement', *Old Kilkenny Review*, new series 2 (1979–83), pp. 329–42, 441–52; T. E. McNeill, *Anglo-Norman Ulster: The History and Archaeology of an Irish Barony 1177–1400* (Edinburgh, 1980), p. 40.
[30] I. W. Rowlands, 'The Making of the March: Aspects of the Norman Settlement in Dyfed', *Proceedings of the Battle Conference*, 3 (1980), 142–59, esp. pp. 146–8; Giraldus Cambrensis, *Speculum Duorum*, ed. M. Richter *et al.* (Cardiff, 1974), p. 37; *Brut*, p. 97 (1220).

its followers, first in England and later in Scotland.[31] These Flemish colonies in the British Isles were, of course, no more than the western branch of a remarkable Flemish diaspora, whose eastern dimension so transformed the German landscape beyond the river Elbe.

Fascinating as are these Flemish communities, what is truly remarkable in the twelfth and thirteenth centuries, and what is in danger of being lost sight of beneath the drum-and-trumpet annals of battles and sieges, is the overflow of English, and for that matter non-English, settlers into outlying parts of the British Isles. If we did not construct our histories so firmly on national lines, if we did not force social developments into a political and military framework, if we were not unduly constrained as we are by the limitations of overwhelmingly ecclesiastical and aristocratic documentation, and if we had not been seduced to such a degree by what has been called (in a different context) 'the myth' of the Normans, we might take a rather different view of what happened in the British Isles in those two centuries. We might view it less as a 'Norman conquest' (though elements of that there were certainly in it), more as the second tidal wave of Anglo-Saxon or English colonization.[32] The first came in the early Middle Ages as soldier-colonists penetrated into the eastern lowlands of Wales and anglicized much of the eastern lowlands of what we know as southern Scotland. The second wave appears to have started in the late eleventh century and flowed more or less strongly over parts of lowland Wales, Ireland and Scotland for almost two centuries. Its dying fall may be represented by two episodes – the peopling of the newly-founded boroughs of north-west Wales and some of the rich valley lands of north-east Wales by English settlers, especially from Shropshire, Cheshire and Lancashire, in the 1280s and 1290s in the wake of Edward I's conquest;[33] and in Ireland the deliberate introduction of 'common' and 'plebeian' English (as the Irish epic dismissively terms them) into Thomas de Clare's newly-granted lands in Thomond, especially into the district around his castle of Bunratty.[34] There can be little doubt that it was this English migration which underpinned what has often been termed the Norman domination of the British Isles. Thus the peoples who settled in the lowlands of Wales were overwhelmingly English, not Norman or Flemish. It was 'Saxons', so the native chronicler tells us, whom Gilbert fitz Richard of Clare brought 'to fill the land' of Ceredigion in the early twelfth century; it is English personal- and field-names which predominate in the earliest land-deeds for 'Norman' Wales in districts such as Brecon, Glamorgan and Gower; it was English which the peasant at Cardiff

[31] Barrow, *Anglo-Norman Era*, pp. 22–3, 38, 44–6, 111–12.

[32] Barrow, *Anglo-Norman Era*, p. 6; W. Davies, *Wales in the Early Middle Ages*, pp. 113, 195.

[33] R. R. Davies, *Lordship and Society in the March of Wales 1284–1400* (Oxford, 1978), pp. 338–48; D. H. Owen, 'The Englishry of Denbigh. An English Colony in Medieval Wales', *Transactions of the Honourable Society of Cymmrodorion*, 1974–5, pp. 57–76.

[34] S. H. O'Grady (ed.), *Caithréim Thoirdhealbhaigh or the Triumphs of Turlogh*, Irish Texts Society, (2 vols. London, 1929), vol. II, pp. 8, 17.

spoke – and which a local knight interpreted – in his altercation with Henry II; while Gerald of Wales – who has precious few kind words to say of the English – remarked that when the crusade was preached at Llandaff the English (*Angli*) stood on one side, the Welsh on the other.[35] And so the evidence could be multiplied.

By the time that Ireland was invaded, the distinction between English and Normans was fast fading within England, as contemporaries themselves recognized. Many of the leaders of the invasion might be classified as 'Norman', 'Anglo-Norman', 'Anglo-French' or 'Cambro-Norman' (all of them terms employed by historians); but the ordinary troops and above all the settlers were overwhelmingly English, with a goodly sprinkling of Welsh and Flemings. It was as 'the English' (*Engleis*) that the newcomers were consistently referred to in the near-contemporary epic of the invasion, *The Song of Dermot and the Earl*; even Gerald, for all his prejudices, was not averse to describing what happened in Ireland as *English* success and *English* domination.[36] Even more significant perhaps – because they are not coloured by rhetoric or the need to make a point – are the references in contemporary documents to 'the conquest of the English' or to 'the arrival of the English and the Welsh in Ireland' as the great watershed in the country's history.[37] The detailed historical evidence of this movement of peoples is late – rarely earlier than the reign of Edward I – but it seems to provide sufficient basis for the claim that 'over wide areas along the east and south coasts (of Ireland), and far inland, there had been ... a substantial immigration of a genuinely peasant population of English, or sometimes Welsh, origin'.[38] It was these peasant and burgess settlers who in the century or so after 1170 transformed the composition of the population of Ireland.

In Scotland the political circumstances were entirely different and so, in many respects, were the social consequences. Some of the characteristic features of Anglo-Norman governance, feudal tenure and aristocratic life were peacefully introduced into Scotland in the twelfth and thirteenth centuries and successfully grafted onto native society. Professor Geoffrey Barrow, in a work of dazzling scholarship, has traced the ancestry of many of the new aristocratic entrepreneurs in Scotland back to England and thence very often, at two or three generations' remove, to Normandy, Flanders or Picardy. This is indeed a remarkable affirmation of 'the Norman achievement', 'that extraordinary and as yet unexplained northern French explosion', at work in Scotland. But

[35] *Brut*, p. 42 (1116); Davies, *Conquest*, pp. 99–100; *Expugnatio*, pp. 108–11 (Bk 1, ch. 40); *Itin. Kambrie*, p. 67 (Bk 1, ch. 7).

[36] *Song*, ll. 467, 476, 491, 510, 529 *et passim*; *Expugnatio*, pp. 70, 80, 232.

[37] N. B. White (ed.), *The 'Dignitas Decani' of St Patrick's Cathedral Dublin*, Irish Manuscripts Commission (Dublin, 1957), p. 113; *Close Rolls 1254–6*, p. 413; A. J. Otway-Ruthven, 'The Character of the Norman Settlement in Ireland', *Historical Studies*, 5 (1965), ed. J. L. McCracken, p. 78.

[38] Otway-Ruthven, *Ireland*, p. 114.

the 'Norman' advance into Scotland was also accompanied, to a degree which cannot be specified because of the nature of the evidence, by English settlement, whether internal migration from within English-speaking Lothian or external migration from Northumberland, Yorkshire and further south into hitherto Celtic-speaking districts such as Upper Tweeddale, Clydesdale and north Ayrshire and also, in even larger numbers, into the newly-founded Scottish burghs.[39] Interestingly enough, when the Gallovidians launched their great revolt in 1174 against the growth of alien domination associated with the king of Scotland, both the English and the French were specifically named as the targets of their wrath. Furthermore the coming of the 'Normans' coincided with, and doubtless contributed towards, the triumph of Englishness and of English speech in much of southern, especially south-eastern, Scotland. The Anglo-Norman settlement, so Professor Barrow concludes, 'greatly reinforced the Middle English elements in Scots speech and culture and had a decisive effect upon the texture of Scottish society as a whole', while for Professor Duncan likewise it is 'the Englishness of the Anglo-Normans' which stands out.[40]

To emphasize the Englishness of the great colonization movement of the twelfth and thirteenth centuries within the British Isles is not to try to score points at the expense of the Normans, nor is it merely to try to draw a semantic distinction where a typical historiographical fudge – such as is represented by the phrase Anglo-Norman or Anglo-French[41] – would do better; it is to try to see the phenomenon in the round and to take away some of the limelight from the military. Without the inflow of colonists, the impact of the Anglo-Normans on Ireland and Wales would have been utterly different. It would have been a political takeover and a military conquest, an act of annexation, no more. But it was very much more. The Anglo-Normans undertook a self-conscious policy of colonization, whether they initiated it or simply channelled a movement which had already generated its own momentum. They set out, in the words of the *Song of Dermot and the Earl*, 'to plant their lands' (*sa terre herberger*), to introduce settlers or *hospites*, or, in the disparaging words of an Irish tract, to inhabit their new conquests with 'common English so many as by bribes and purchase' they were able to attract.[42] They recognized that without such settlements there would be no depth to their achievement; as a memorandum to the royal council in 1350 put it, there was little point in pouring huge sums into war against the Irish; it was far better to conquer land from the enemy and to inhabit it with English

[39] Barrow, *Anglo-Norman Era*, pp. 9, 30, 48–9, 107.

[40] W. Stubbs (ed.), *Gesta Regis Henrici Secundi*, Rolls Series (2 vols. London, 1867), vol. II, pp. 67–8; Barrow, *Anglo-Norman Era*, p. 117; A. A. M. Duncan in *Times Literary Supplement*, 20 November 1981, p. 1369.

[41] K. W. Nichols has urged the adoption of this phrase in 'Anglo-French Ireland and After', *Peritia*, 1 (1982), pp. 370–403.

[42] *Song*, l. 2941; *CDI*, vol. I, nos. 120, 886, 1677; *Caithréim*, vol. II, p. 8.

settlers.[43] Similarly in Wales English families were enticed to settle both in the countryside and in the new plantation boroughs on highly attractive and favourable terms. The strategic as well as the economic aspect of such colonization was occasionally specifically indicated in later evidence, as in the direction given to the custodian of Glamorgan to remove the Welsh from the plains and to install Englishmen there for the greater safety of the land, or in the encouragement given to Englishmen in north Wales to secure the leases of Welsh land 'so that the peace will be assured and security improved by Englishmen so placed'.[44] The end result of such a policy of colonization was to create substantial (at least in relation to existing population levels) colonies of settlers, mainly English by descent and speech, in outlying parts of the British Isles. They could, as in parts of lowland Scotland, merge into and transform existing societies especially where, as in Lothian, they were kindred to them in social structure and language. In much of Ireland and Wales, however, these communities remained defiantly separate, cowering under the skirts of their military protectors and sponsors, jealously protective of their privileges and status. When those communities emerge into the fuller light of historical day, it is as 'the *English* community of Glamorgan' or 'the *English* people of the county of Pembroke' or the '*English* nation' or '*English* liege people' in Ireland that they proudly identified themselves.[45] By then English national identity had become much more clearly and aggressively defined; the defence of the English communities in Wales and Ireland against the natives on the one hand and against a seemingly inexorable process of 'degeneracy', as it was called, on the other – that is, the assimilation of the settlers into their native habitat and their adoption of its customs – was represented as the defence of a specifically *English* culture. To say so is, of course, to anticipate and to short-circuit a historical process which gradually unfolds during the thirteenth century.[46] Yet the occasionally intolerant Englishness of settler communities in Wales and Ireland in the later Middle Ages was, indirectly, a belated comment on the wave of English colonization which swept over some of the outlying lowlands of the British Isles in the two centuries after 1100. These communities and their attitudes and affiliations were the essential infrastructure of the edifice of domination; they were not a secondary or incidental adjunct to it.

Even without such colonization, however, it is clear that Ireland, Scotland and Wales would have been increasingly drawn – and indeed were so drawn –

[43] Sayles (ed.), *Affairs of Ireland*, p. 193.
[44] *Calendar of Chancery Warrants 1244–1326* (London, 1927), p. 448; *Calendar of Close Rolls 1339–41*, p. 251.
[45] W. Rees (ed.), *Calendar of Ancient Petitions relating to Wales* (Cardiff, 1975), nos. 7356, 8242, 13029; *Rotuli Parliamentorum*, Record Commission (7 vols., London 1783–1832), vol. III, p. 518; Sayles (ed.), *Affairs of Ireland*, pp. 224–6; H. F. Berry (ed.), *Statutes, Ordinances and Acts of the Parliament of Ireland, John–Henry V* (Dublin, 1907), p. 343.
[46] R. R. Davies, 'Lordship or Colony?' in James Lydon (ed.), *The English in Medieval Ireland* (Dublin, 1984), pp. 142–60.

into a European and specifically a north-west European, Anglo-Norman culture orbit in this very period. Acculturation can be an enriching experience; it brings one culture and its values into contact with another; it revivifies and redirects cultural energies. But it can also be an insidiously destructive experience, especially for the minority or subservient culture and for the political and social order which is associated with it.[47] This is particularly so when the intrusive culture is aligned, consciously or otherwise, with the ambitions of an acquisitive kingship and aristocracy, a centralizing church and a proselytizing and categorizing clerical élite. The status of the existing culture is drained of its authority, and with its decline the political structure which sustained it, and was sustained by it, is undermined. Such was the common situation on the borders of Europe in the twelfth and thirteenth centuries, whether on the Elbe or in Spain, Brittany, Wales or Ireland. This cultural challenge in its broadest sense is surely part of the essential context of the mentality of domination.

We may start our very brief review of it with the Church. Imbued as our historiography is – or until recently was – with notions of a 'Celtic church' and by a chronology which often ties ecclesiastical developments to the coat-tails of political history, it is natural to explain changes in the Church in terms of the impact of invasion and external domination. Such a view was indeed actively encouraged by the conquerors, anxious as they were to explain and justify their activities, in part at least, as a campaign of ecclesiastical reform and spiritual regeneration. It is a claim which can by no means be altogether gainsaid; but equally, and more importantly in the present context, it cannot by any means be entirely conceded. The Church in Europe awoke with a start to its international responsibilities and opportunities in the eleventh and twelfth centuries, notably through what historians call, by way of shorthand, the papal reform movement and the monastic revival. The impact of this papal and monastic revolution was to make Europe a much more international, compact, integrated and uniform continent ecclesiastically by 1200 than, arguably, it had been before or has been since. Ireland, Scotland and Wales were at a considerable distance from a movement whose epicentres lay in Rome, Cluny, Tiron, Savigny or Cîteaux; but they were by no means immune from its impact. That impact, it should be emphasized, was not necessarily dependent on external political domination or military conquest.[48] Papal legates, native or *a latere*, presided over reforming synods; appeals were dispatched to Rome; prelates from Ireland and Wales picked up the habit of foreign travel; and native churchmen began to measure the health (or more

---

[47] See in general D. Kaplan, 'The Law of Cultural Dominance', in M. D. Sahlins and E. R. Service (eds.), *Evolution and Culture* (Michigan, 1960), pp. 69–92; Philip Mason, *Patterns of Dominance* (Oxford, 1971).

[48] Huw Pryce, 'Church and Society in Wales, 1150–1250: An Irish Perspective', in R. R. Davies (ed.), *The British Isles 1100–1500. Comparisons, Contrasts and Connections* (Edinburgh, 1988), pp. 27–47.

often the sickness) of their local churches by what they perceived to be centrally-agreed norms of ecclesiastical conduct and governance. The tide of continental monastic reform likewise washed over the 'Celtic' countries and did so independently of any Norman conquest. Three examples may serve to typify this movement: in 1113 David (the future king) of Scotland (1124–53), who was himself to visit Tiron in 1116, founded a monastery at Selkirk (later to be transferred to Kelso) and invited a body of monks from Tiron to establish their rule there; in 1142 Bernard of Clairvaux dispatched a mixed group of French and Irish monks to found the first Cistercian monastery in Ireland at Mellifont; while a generation later Lord Rhys (d. 1197), the victorious ruler of Deheubarth in Wales, took over the patronage of the recently-established Cistercian monastery of Strata Florida and was munificent in his support of it, not least from the lands of former Welsh religious communities.

The 'Celtic' countries of the British Isles were responding enthusiastically to the challenge and opportunities of ecclesiastical reform and doing so, as it were, of their own accord and independently of Anglo-Norman impetus and political power. Yet in an analysis of the character of domination, two consequences of this movement may be worth noting. Reforming churchmen in Wales and Ireland were now committed to what we may call an alternative ecclesiastical culture, an international code of norms, conduct, institutions and contacts which distanced them in a degree from the cultural affiliations and even the political links with their own native societies. The Irish ecclesiastical hierarchy showed as much when it submitted to Henry II in 1171–2 and attended the council he summoned at Cashel – quite simply because they saw him as a ruler who might sponsor and speed up the reforming process within the church. Likewise in Wales the bishops of Bangor and St Asaph, even when they were Welsh, frequently found their zeal for reform and their respect for the conventions of an international church stronger than any loyalty they may have felt for the native Welsh princes. Secondly, though the ecclesiastical reform movement was truly international, it was in some measure mediated through Anglo-Norman experience and exemplars. Thus, to give a few examples, it was from Furness in Lancashire that the first Savignac house was founded in Ireland in 1127; it was under the tutelage of Combermere in Cheshire and, subsequently, of Buildwas in Shropshire that the abbey of St Mary's Dublin was placed long before the coming of the Normans to Ireland; while it was monks from Lanfranc's reformed monastery at Canterbury whom Queen Margaret chose to man her Benedictine priory at Dunfermline. There is, of course, nothing inherently 'national' or sinister in such links; but even contemporaries recognized that political ambitions might be promoted, consciously or otherwise, under the banner of ecclesiastical reform. It was Gerald of Wales – in his salad days before the frustrations of his own career soured his judgement – who perhaps gave the game away most openly when he added a gloss to his report on the synod of Cashel in 1172 that henceforth 'in all parts of the Irish church all matters ... are to be conducted hereafter ... in line with the observances of the English church'.[49] Ireland had at least escaped out of the reach of the metropolitan clutches of Canterbury. Not so Wales, and it was Gerald – now speaking from the depth of his own personal frustrations and bitterness – who commented shrewdly but sourly that Canterbury's metropolitan jurisdiction in Wales was used as the spiritual arm of the English king's political domination there. Ecclesiastical conformity, political domination and English usage were dangerously close partners. Even in Scotland – where English pretensions to metropolitan control were, with Papal help, firmly rebuffed – the impact of the English model was remarkably influential in matters such as liturgical usage, ecclesiastical constitutions and even architecture. So much so that Professor Duncan has concluded that 'the Scottish church derived its most immediate experience of Latin Christianity from the church in England.'[50]

What was true of the church and religion applies to culture in the broadest sense of that word. Just as the papacy and international monastic orders came to dominate church life throughout Europe, so in the aristocratic and academic world France came to exercise a quite exceptional dominance. 'Our books', so remarked Chrétien of Troyes with pride bordering on smugness, 'have informed us that pre-eminence in chivalry and learning once belonged to Greece. Then chivalry passed to Rome. Together with the highest learning it has now come to France.'[51] Such was the supremacy of this 'French' culture that even the outlying parts of the British Isles were sucked into its vortex. The evidence is ample if very fragmentary and occasionally difficult to interpret; it can only be hinted at here. Scholars travelled to Europe: the chief lector at Armagh from the 1150s, so the Annals of Ulster tell us, had pursued his studies for twenty-one years in France and England; while Gerald of Wales met two youths from the diocese of St Davids at school in France on one of his journeys in Europe.[52] French learning and habits were pervasive in their impact. Thus several hundred words were assimilated into medieval Welsh from French, whether directly or alternatively though Anglo-Norman or middle English borrowings, and the topics of borrowed words – notably aristocratic and commercial life – indicate the most obvious and significant points of contact in

[49] *Expugnatio*, pp. 100 (Bk 1, ch. 35); 142 (Bk 2, ch. 5 'according to the usage of the church in England'). Ralph de Diceto in his *Opera Historica* (ed. W. Stubbs, Rolls Series (London, 1876) vol. I, pp. 350–1) likewise refers to 'marriage customs which are accepted and observed in England'.
[50] Duncan, *Scotland*, p. 283.
[51] Quoted in Colin Morris, *The Discovery of the Individual 1050–1200* (London, 1972), p. 37.
[52] Katharine Simms, *From Kings to Warlords. The Changing Political Structure of Gaelic Ireland in the Later Middle Ages* (Woodbridge, 1987), p. 12; H. Butler (ed.), *Autobiography of Gerald of Wales*, pp. 162–3.

this system of acculturation.[53] Native Welsh literature began to borrow some of its topoi, motifs and terminology from French aristocratic culture and broadened its acquaintance with that culture by translations of some of its classical texts, notably *The Song of Roland*. Nowhere was this literary cross-fertilization more obvious than in the work of Geoffrey of Monmouth and the response to it. Geoffrey pillaged native Welsh and Breton lore for his own purposes; but even more significant for the present argument is the way in which Geoffrey's fabrications, along with aspects of the Matters of France and Rome, were integrated into the corpus of traditional Welsh learning.[54] Such was the status and seductiveness of this new international culture. Much the same was true of architecture and sculpture; continental and English models were already proving influential well before the Anglo-Norman troops marched in, as the examples of Cormac's Chapel at Cashel (consecrated in 1134) or Boyle Abbey (co. Roscommon) suggest. Once political and military domination was secured, those models became even more influential. 'Between 1200 and 1250', it has been said, 'there must have been an almost constant flow of experienced masons making the voyage across the Irish Sea and by the middle of the century the Early English style was *de rigeur* throughout the island'.[55]

There was, of course, no wholesale surrender of native traditions and cultural norms; indeed in many directions it is the remarkable conservatism, resilience and adaptive qualities of native literary and legal learning which stand out, especially in Ireland and Wales. Yet the world could never be the same again. A confident, expansive, exciting and rich international culture had come to occupy centre stage in northern Europe; its drawing-power and its enticing supremacy were irresistible. Indeed those who dared to withstand its charms could be dismissed as barbarians: when Stephen of Lexington, dispatched to investigate Cistercian observance in Ireland, decreed that knowledge of French or Latin was a prerequisite for a monk and added, crushingly, that 'no man can love the cloister and learning if he knows only Irish', he was proclaiming the values of a European cultural and religious world into which the 'Celtic' countries were being dragged willy nilly.[56] Some of them, indeed, were being dragged there enthusiastically and with almost unseemly speed. A contemporary observer remarked that William the Lion of Scotland (1165–1214) 'cherished, loved and held dear people from abroad. He never had much affection for those of his own country'. An English chronicler

[53] M. Surridge, 'Romance Linguistic Influence on Middle Welsh', *Studia Celtica*, 1 (1966), pp. 63–93.
[54] Bromwich (ed.), *Trioedd Ynys Prydein*, pp. lxxviii–lxxxi; B. F. Roberts, 'Geoffrey of Monmouth and Welsh Historical Tradition', *Nottingham Medieval Studies*, 20 (1976), 29–40.
[55] Roger Stalley, 'Irish Gothic and English fashion' in Lydon (ed.), *English in Medieval Ireland*, p. 75.
[56] Quoted in Watt, *The Church and the Two Nations*, p. 96, n. 1.

was more restrained but more acute in his analysis: 'the more recent Scottish kings count themselves Frenchmen by race (*genere*), manners, habit and speech and retain Frenchmen only in their service and following'.[57]

A powerful wave of French cultural domination was sweeping across the British Isles, especially at the higher levels of church aristocracy. It is important to emphasize that it was a French or European, not an English, wave: Stephen of Lexington, Englishman that he was, ended his career as abbot of Clairvaux and it was French or Latin, not English, which he made the linguistic *sine qua non* for the monastic life. Nevertheless, cultural dominance and a measure of political dependence, however genteel its forms, are often not unconnected. It was to a very considerable degree through the courts of the Norman and Angevin kings of England and their aristocracies, through the households of English bishops or through English monasteries that European learning and norms were mediated. Gerald of Wales noted how Welshmen – and the same was doubtless true of Irish and Scots – had their eyes opened to this new world and its values through visits, be they social or custodial, to the king of England's court.[58] Interpreters – Morice Regan, interpreter and secretary to King Diarmait Mac Murchada, who provided the author of *The Song of Dermot and the Earl* with his material is an example – opened their eyes further.[59] At a provincial level local courts – such as those of Gilbert, earl of Strathearn (whose wife was an Aubigni) or the princes of Powys who frequently chose their consorts from the Norman families of the English border counties – doubtless further promoted the process of acculturation.[60] It was often at the coat-tails of the Anglo-Normans and along the channels of peaceful contact rather than at the point of the sword that continental influences reached the outlying parts of the British Isles. The point need not be laboured or pressed too far; but it is clear that French cultural domination was by no means necessarily politically neutral. Within the British Isles it was a cultural domination which was bound to be closely associated with the political and ecclesiastical masters of England.

Nor is that all. Like other dominant cultures, that of northern Europe in the twelfth century was not only confident, it was also often morally and intellectually superior in its attitude towards other cultures. These cultures were approached and categorized in an attitude which ranged from supercilious curiosity to outright condemnation. Such categorization is in itself an act of domination; indeed it provides an invaluable insight into the

57 R. C. Johnston (ed.), *Jordan Fantosme's Chronicle* (Oxford, 1981), pp. 48–9; W. Stubbs (ed.), *Memoriale Fratris Walteri de Coventria*, Rolls Series (2 vols., London 1872–3), vol. II, p. 206.
58 *Descr. Kambrie*, p. 218 (Bk 2, ch. 7).
59 Joseph Long, 'Dermot and the Earl: who wrote "the Song"', *Proceedings of the Royal Irish Academy*, 75 (1975), Section C, pp. 263–72; Constance Bullock-Davies, *Professional Interpreters and the Matter of Britain* (Cardiff, 1966).
60 Duncan, *Scotland*, pp. 448–9; Davies, *Conquest*, pp. 102, 233.

thought-world of the dominating élite. For how men see the world, and in particular how they view themselves and their relationship to others, provides the essential context for their actions. Nowhere more so than in the British Isles in the twelfth and thirteenth centuries. The cultures and societies of Wales and Ireland and to a far lesser extent Scotland were weighed in the balance of European norms, as defined by the academics and ecclesiastics of the day, and were found to be hopelessly wanting, even if some of their virtues attracted the praise that is often directed towards the noble savage and the values of 'primitive' societies.[61] Condemnation may be said in particular and in brief to concentrate on three issues. First, these societies were economically underdeveloped and indeed culpably backward. Their agriculture was primitive and pastoral; town life, trade and money were more or less absent; forms of economic exploitation and exchange were primitive. 'The soil of Ireland', as William of Newburgh put it, 'would be fertile, if it did not lack the industry of a capable farmer; but the people are rough and barbarous in their ways . . . and lazy in agriculture'.[62] For William – as for so many commentators in generations to come – defects of character were the obvious explanation for economic backwardness. Secondly, these societies were politically immature. The Welsh, it was remarked, were incapable of obeying anyone and seemed to exult in an anarchic love of liberty; the Irish were no better since 'no public authority was constituted among them'.[63] Neither recognized the benefits of unitary rule; in both countries the units of political power were small and fluid, for as *The Song of Dermot and the Earl* remarked, 'kings were as multiple in Ireland as were counts (or earls) elsewhere'.[64] The results were obvious and were readily characterized by contemporaries: 'mutual slaughter'; 'universal discord'; absence of peace; lack of law and statutes; a political volatility and unreliability evident both within the societies themselves as well as in their external relations.[65] Thirdly, the social customs and moral, sexual and marital habits of these societies showed that they were at best at an early stage of social evolution (as both William of Newburgh and Gerald of Wales in different contexts suggested), at worst that 'this barbarous nation', as the Pope had it of the Irish, was 'Christian only in name', and was, as St Bernard had averred, in

---

[61] R. Bartlett, *Gerald of Wales 1146–1223* (Oxford, 1982), pp. 158–77; W. R. Jones, 'The Image of the Barbarian in Medieval Europe', *Comparative Studies in Society and History*, 13 (1971), pp. 376–407; *idem*, 'England against the Celtic Fringe: A Study in Cultural Sterotypes', *Journal of World History*, 13 (1971), pp. 155–71.

[62] William of Newburgh, 'Historia', vol. i, pp. 165–6.

[63] Quoted in Glanmor Williams, *The Welsh Church from Conquest to Reformation*, 2nd edn. (Cardiff, 1976), p. 398; Ralph de Diceto, *Opera Historica*, vol. i, p. 350.

[64] *Song*, ll. 2191–2.

[65] Ralph de Diceto, *Opera Historica*, vol. i, p. 350; *Gesta Stephani*, eds. K. R. Potter and R. H. C. Davis (Oxford, 1976), pp. 9, 20; J. A. Watt, *The Church in Medieval Ireland* (Dublin, 1972) p. 37.

fact pagan.[66] The evidence for such a charge was ample, ranging from the delight of the Welsh and Irish in dangerously outdated virtues such as family vengeance and feud (which led them to be 'prodigal of life' to an exceptional degree) to their flouting of the church's social teaching on issues such as cohabitation before marriage, concubinage, divorce, the fostering out of children, and the status of children born out of wedlock.

The creation of these stereotyped images of the Welsh and the Irish (and later, within Scotland, of the Highlanders)[67] are of great interest in the study of the mentality of domination. As so often with such images they tell us as much, if not more, about the world of the image-makers as about the societies they are attempting to characterize. The images, created as they were by an ecclesiastical and intellectual élite, speak to us of a Europe where a set of international norms was being established on acceptable social and sexual morality, political organization and relationships, economic structures and forms of exploitation and even on matters such as clothes, food, housing and the forms of settlement. The interrelation of this package of norms is occasionally revealed in such give-away comments as Raoul Glaber's observation that the wealth of the Bretons consisted in 'freedom from taxes and abundance of milk' and William of Poitiers' devastating criticism, again of the Bretons, that they 'do not engage in the cultivation of fields or of good morals' – as if arable farming and clean living went together.[68] An image of a civilized society had been created and so by contrast had an image of an underdeveloped, or as they would have said barbarian, society. Such images facilitated domination. Domination is more readily justified and explained if the difference between the dominant and subordinate groups, the conquerors and the conquered, is exaggerated. Gerald classified Wales as a barbarian society (*regio barbara*) and would certainly have included Ireland in that category; England, on the other hand, was a well-ordered society (*regio composita*).[69] It is a classification which speaks volumes to us of the world of Gerald, his contemporaries and his kinsmen, the conquerors of Ireland.

Men so confident of their classifications and of their superiority were likely to be imbued with a civilizing mission, a duty to introduce their values and norms – political, economic, moral and ecclesiastical – to less fortunate peoples, especially those who were nominally Christian. Churchmen were, of course, most eloquent on that score; like all clerics and intellectuals, they had a professional habit of covering their actions under a cloak of righteousness. But their views influenced and no doubt refracted

[66] *Expugnatio*, p. 146 (Bk 2, ch. 5); Watt, *Church in Medieval Ireland*, p. 17.
[67] For the emergence of the stereotype of the Highlanders see A. Grant, *Independence and Nationhood. Scotland 1306–1469* (London, 1984), pp. 200–6.
[68] Quoted in Bartlett, *Gerald of Wales*, pp. 160–1.
[69] Quoted in Bartlett, *Gerald of Wales*, p. 205.

those of their lay colleagues. 'The Normans', so remarked one chronicler, 'perseveringly civilized Wales; ... they made the land so productive and abounding in all resources that you would have considered it in no wise inferior to the most fertile part of Britain.'[70] Later another contemporary took much the same view of Henry II's achievements in Brittany: he 'expelled and overawed troublemakers and so arranged and ruled the whole of the province that the people could work peacefully and land hitherto deserted be brought into cultivation'.[71] When we speak of domination, we should be ready to concede that to some contemporaries at least what was involved was providing the opportunity for political order and economic development and for dragging societies such as Wales and Ireland into the modern, civilized world. It is a familiar enough aspect of the imperial mission; it should not for that reason be discounted or dismissed.

There is a final aspect of the stereotyped images of backward societies which should be mentioned. The images, at least as they survive in the historical evidence, are intellectual constructs created by clerics trained in the schools. They are part of the legacy of an academic–clerical society increasingly confident of the power of its own logic and reason and of the universality and orthodoxy of its normative values. It was a society which was becoming increasingly dogmatic and intolerant of deviations from its standards.[72] The images of a barbarian society it created were, in J. L. Austin's famous phrase, part of the things it did with words, as all societies do. The impact of such ideas on men's way of thinking and acting should not be underestimated. The concept of the barbarian and the categories it implied were already in place by the time Wales was invaded and long before the invasion of Ireland was planned. These categories and concepts justified the invasions, while the invasions in turn confirmed the categories and concepts. In other words, the ideological basis for domination had already been shaped.

That is not to claim that there is a simple direct line from thought to action; but it is to claim that we must try to see the process of domination in the round. It has too long been controlled by the chronology of conquest and by the viewpoint of military men. Military power was, of course, crucial; but a good measure of domination could be achieved without it. Furthermore, on any long-term view what is remarkable about the British Isles is how loath many Anglo-Normans were to embark on conquest. Thus the conquest of Wales was a slow and hesitant process which took over two centuries to be completed. Norman observer and Welsh chronicler alike might have written

---

[70] *Gesta Stephani*, p. 9.   [71] William of Newburgh, 'Historia', vol. i, pp. 146–7.
[72] See in general A. Murray, *Reason and Society in the Middle Ages*, ch. 5; and R. I. Moore, *The Formation of a Persecuting Society: Power and Deviance in Western Europe*, 950–1250 (Oxford, 1987).

Wales off as a viable political unit in the 1090s;[73] but for much of the twelfth and thirteenth centuries the kings of England seemed neither capable nor anxious to deliver the *coup de grâce*. As for Ireland, what is surely remarkable is how slow the Anglo-Normans were to take up the opportunity and challenge of conquest, in spite of an occasional flexing of muscles in the century before 1169. Furthermore when the invasion did take place it was by native invitation, and it proved to be an invasion which very rapidly earned the stern disapproval of the king of England. As for Scotland, its history in the early twelfth century showed clearly that effective political tutelage and a deep aristocratic penetration could be achieved without military confrontation, let alone conquest. Periods of high tension there might be in Anglo-Scottish relations; but anything that could be called a conquest was not attempted until the high-handedness and single-mindedness of Edward I drove him to it (though the English barons had boasted earlier that they could smash the Scots without the help of anyone).[74] All this hardly suggests a mighty appetite for conquest; what it does suggest is that there might be alternative routes to domination. Domination is a much more subtle, rich-textured and many-faceted process than an over-concentration on the military story line of conquest might suggest.

[73] *Brut*, p. 19; Florence of Worcester, *Chronicon ex Chronicis*, ed. B. Thorpe, English Historical Society (2 vols., London, 1848), vol. ii, p. 31.
[74] Matthew Paris, *Chronica Majora*, ed. H. R. Luard, Rolls Series (7 vols., London 1872–83), vol. iv, p. 278.

2

Aristocratic domination

Our historical vision is unduly narrowed, so it was claimed in the previous chapter, by concentrating too exclusively on the story of conquest and its accompanying chronology. We are thereby in danger of according the military a higher profile than it deserves in the history of the Anglo-Norman domination of the British Isles. To contemporaries, the Anglo-Norman conquest did not have the overwhelming inevitability which it has naturally come to enjoy with hindsight. For example, in the native Welsh annals, written it is true in west Wales, the Normans are only mentioned thrice before 1093; to the annalist they took second place to the Vikings. Nor is that surprising, since the Vikings had devastated St Davids in 1073 and killed its bishop on a further raid in 1080. In Ireland, the initial arrival of the Anglo-Normans prompted equally small surprise: 'A strong force of knights came to Mac Murchada' was the pithy comment of one annalist. Indeed there are indications that Mac Murchada may have believed – or at least persuaded others to believe – that once the 'foreigners' had restored him to his position in Leinster, they would be asked to leave.[1] Furthermore, it is doubtful whether the Welsh or the Irish saw the Anglo-Normans at first as 'conquerors'. They themselves, or some of them, had invited them as allies, just as earlier they had invited Vikings, Anglo-Saxons or Irish; they looked to them for support and protection for their own ends; they assimilated their relationships with them – in gift-giving, payment of tribute, handing over of hostages and so forth – to the pattern of relationships already familiar to them in the native politics of Wales and Ireland. The Anglo-Normans, for their part, often established their domination by relatively peaceful means, scarcely doing more than baring their military teeth (as William the Conqueror did in Scotland in 1072 or south Wales in 1081), or offering themselves as allies or mercenaries to native princes and pretenders, or easing their passage comfortably into the host society by a well-chosen marriage. The Anglo-Normans in other words were more than a military master-race; they secured their domination by whatever route was simplest, cheapest and best-suited to their ends; their path to mastery and the

[1] *NHI*, vol. II, p.l; *Expugnatio*, p. 50 (Bk 1, ch. 10).

25

nature of their penetration varied greatly according to time, place and opportunity.

It is small wonder, therefore, that historians both in Wales and Ireland have of late doubted the appropriateness of terms such as 'invasion' and 'conquest' to describe the coming of the Anglo-Normans.[2] Evidence is not lacking to support their point of view. In districts such as Gwent in south-east Wales and Desmond in south-west Ireland the incomers seem almost to have sidled into the country, often apparently meeting little resistance and sometimes arriving by invitation; while elsewhere the Anglo-Normans appear to have done little more than give a stir to the already turbulent pot that was native politics. 'At first', as one Irish historian has appropriately observed, 'the Normans simply added a cutting-edge to the attacks of old enemies.'[3]

But the cutting-edge of the Normans was razor-sharp, devastatingly superior in its military technology, and, where necessary, horrifyingly brutal. The Norman seizure of power was certainly no genteel take-over. English historians (especially, perhaps, those who study southern England), may occasionally seem to give the impression that it was so in England, averting their eyes from brutality in favour of the cultivation of Domesday statistics and learned arguments about institutional continuity and the origins of feudalism. Contemporaries themselves, even Norman apologists, were under no illusions. Orderic Vitalis, for example, had no hesitation in referring to 'the foreign robbers, supporters of the victorious William', despoiling the country; while William of Malmesbury spoke with profound sorrow of an England which was 'the habitation of strangers and the domination of foreigners' and of 'the newcomers who devour its riches and entrails'.[4] Welsh and Irish historians are forced to live much longer with the grim military realities of the Anglo-Norman take-over, if only for the obvious reason that in both Wales and Ireland the story of conquest was long-drawn-out and inconclusive, re-fuelled in each generation by grisly new massacres. Even the Norman historians themselves blenched at the blood-lust and tyranny of the *conquistadores*: William fitz Osbern, earl of Hereford, so Orderic tells us, 'caused the ruin and wretched deaths of many thousands'; his near contemporary, the earl of Shrewsbury, visited his psychopathic brutality – *immania* is the chronicler's word – on the Welsh for four years; even at St Evroul, the monastery in Normandy on which he had visited his generosity, Robert of Rhuddlan, the earl of Chester's lieutenant in north Wales, was remembered for his 'un-

[2] See for example F. X. Martin in *NHI*, vol. II, pp. 43–5; D. Crouch, 'The Slow Death of Kingship in Glamorgan 1067–1158', *Morgannwg*, 29 (1985), pp. 20–41; P. Courtney, 'The Norman invasion of Gwent: a reassessment', *Journal of Medieval History*, 12 (1986), pp. 297–313.
[3] K. Simms, 'The O Hanlons, the O Neills and the Anglo-Normans in Thirteenth-Century Armagh', *Seanchas Ard Mhacha*, 9 (1978–9), 74.
[4] Orderic Vitalis, *Historia Ecclesiastica*, ed. M. Chibnall (6 vols., Oxford, 1969–80), vol. II, pp. 190, 266; William of Malmesbury, *De Gestis Regum* vol. I, p. 278.

restrained plunder and slaughter'; while even those Irish historians, whose historical stomachs have been fortified against squeamishness by taking the native annals as their bedside reading, must surely feel that some of the episodes of the English conquest of Ireland – such as the massacre of the citizens of Waterford and the catapulting of their bodies, whether dead or alive, over the cliffs – reach new levels of nauseating horror.[5]

The impact of such a military *blitzkrieg* on the profoundly conservative and hierarchic societies of Wales and Ireland, and especially on their ruling élites, must have been traumatic. By the 1090s the native sources in Wales begin to register loud and clear their dawning realization that their world was collapsing around them. Outrage was quickly replaced by apocalyptic fear. The annalist remarked that 'the tyranny, injustice, violence and oppression of the French' were unbearable; the colonists who accompanied them 'drove away all the inhabitants from the land'; their king had allegedly introduced the draconian measure that 'no one was to dwell in Ceredigion, neither natives nor strangers'; while his intention, and that of his barons, was nothing less than genocidal, 'the extermination of all the Britons, so that the name of the Britons should never more be called to mind from that time forth'.[6] The tone of a remarkable Latin poem written in the 1090s by the scholar-cleric Rhigyfarch was in no doubt that his whole world was collapsing around him socially, culturally and morally. His despair was utter: 'Why have the blind fates not let us die? ... O [Wales] you are afflicted and dying'.[7] Such passages are not merely flights of rhetoric; they register for us some of the psychological trauma of defeat at the hands of the Anglo-Normans. The Welsh and the Irish were long used to wars and battles and defeats; but the victory of the Anglo-Normans was different. It brought with it a threat to, if not the imminent collapse of, a whole world of values, relationships and priorities, especially for the aristocratic and clerical élites. It disrupted the ordered pattern of nature and society; that is why Rhigyfarch saw it as life-threatening.

The despair of the Welsh and the Irish was matched by the sense of adventure and thrill felt by the Anglo-Normans. Here the historian is ill-served both by his sources and by himself. Most of his sources are clerical in provenance and are suffused by the need to provide ecclesiastical justification and a measure of *ex post facto* rationalization, in other words by what Marc Bloch called, perhaps rather unkindly, 'a veneer of disingenuousness'.[8] Historians for their part are quiet people, much given to contemplation and explanation and to the exercise of what Carlyle called dismissively their

---

[5] Orderic Vitalis, *Historia Ecclesiastica*, vol. ii, pp. 318–21; vol. v, pp. 224–5; vol. iv, pp. 138–9; *Expugnatio*, pp. 58–65 (Bk 1, chs. 14–15); *Song*, ll. 1474–89.

[6] *Brut*, pp. 19, 27, 31, 37; *Brut (RBH)*, p. 39.

[7] M. Lapidge, 'The Welsh-Latin Poetry of Sulien's Family', *Studia Celtica*, 8–9 (1973–4), 91. For a contemporary Irish poetical reaction to the invaders see B. Ó Cuív, 'A poem composed for Cathal Croibdhearg Ó Conchubhair', *Ériu*, 34 (1983), pp. 157–74.

[8] M. Bloch, *Feudal Society*, trans. L. A. Manyon (London, 1961), p. 80.

'Logical and Commensurative faculties'. They are thereby ill-fitted to come to terms with the Anglo-Norman conquerors – men of instinct, impetuousness and action, men of high emotion and proudly violent passions. Wales, Scotland and Ireland were but small corners of the huge arena in which these men exercised their congenital restlessness in the eleventh and twelfth centuries. The momentum behind that restlessness still defies a convincing analysis; what is obvious, however, is that we must not be too crudely determinist or too calculatingly economic in our explanations. These warriors themselves, after all, did not know the end of the story or what success would attend their enterprises. They wanted quick returns and if they did not get them they would sell their services to other masters or head for home. Such, for example, so *The Song of Dermot and the Earl* tells us, was the reaction of one of the early Anglo-Norman adventurers in Ireland, Maurice of Prender-gast (or of Ossory, as he came to be known), though in the event he sold his services to an Irish king, for money and for a specified period.[9] Others retired into religious houses and so became drop-outs from the saga of conquest: Wethenoc of Monmouth and Hervey de Montmorency are well-known Welsh and Irish examples. Others lost their military appetites: one Anglo-Norman knight abandoned his manor on the frontiers of Wales because, in an unusually frank admission, 'he could not hold it peacefully against the Welsh because of his want of weight and power'.[10] Some were so appalled by the habits and living conditions of the Irish and the Welsh that they retired in horrified disgust – sharing the views of the Shropshire monk who, cooped up in a dug-out oak tree which was the best he could do for a hotel in Dunbrody (co. Wexford), wrote home in despair about 'the desolation of the place, the sterility of the soil and the wildness and ferociousness of the inhabitants'.[11] Others were hoodwinked by the misinformation deliberately fed them by natives: such was the Breton knight who was persuaded by a wily local cleric that the Welsh were forced to live on roots and grasses and who accordingly reported back to the king that the country was fit only for a bestial race of people.[12] The men most difficult to trace are precisely those who did not put down roots in the new countries. We should not overlook them for that reason.

Equally we should not underestimate the element of military adventure, of sheer kicks, involved in these enterprises. Our own essentially peace-oriented instincts and the overwhelmingly territorial character of contemporary documentation might well mislead us here. It is through their land charters that we generally see these men (in so far as we can trace them at all); that may well

[9] *Song*, ll. 1070–95, 1274–80, 1342–7. Cf. *Expugnatio*, p. 134 (Bk 2, ch. 1).
[10] *Calendar of Inquisitions Miscellaneous* (7 vols. London, 1916–68), vol. I, no. 1059.
[11] *Chart. St Mary's Dublin*, vol. I, pp. 354–5. Professor James Lydon first drew my attention to this report.
[12] *Itin. Kambrie*, pp. 81–2 (Bk 1, ch. 10).

lead us to under-rate other aspects of their lives and ambitions. It was as 'noble and courteous knights', in the words of the *Song of Dermot and the Earl*, that they cared to think of themselves, at least in their better moments. What often motivated them, as was said of Meiler fitz Henry, was 'love of praise and glory; all his actions were related to that end'.[13] Such praise and glory in the chivalric world came, of course, primarily from military feats of prowess. That is why, for example, the most flattering obituaries that the family chronicler could pen for a succession of Mortimers were those of 'a valiant conqueror of the Welsh' or 'a warlike and vigorous man . . . who tamed the ferocity of the Welsh'.[14] It was military memories above all others which these men and their families treasured. The desperate siege of the tiny castle at Pembroke in the 1090s could be vividly (perhaps too vividly) recalled by Gerald of Wales almost a century later. He recounted how his grandfather, in a calculated act of bravado, threw his last supplies to the besiegers and wrote a spoof letter, which by design fell into the hands of the Welsh, announcing that he did not need help for several months hence. Memories of such daring acts were carefully preserved and frequently savoured in these militarist frontier societies. What such men feared above all was military dishonour and disgrace. 'Let it not appear, my friend', so Strongbow is alleged to have remarked, 'that our men are brought to shame'. Memories of shame lived long to haunt men. Side by side with the bravado of his grandfather, Gerald recalled how fifteen knights, terrified by the odds against them in the same siege of Pembroke in the 1090s, tried to escape by boat; their ignominious penalty was the forfeiture of their arms and estates and the grant of both, along with the belt of knighthood, to their squires.[15]

It may, of course, be objected that idealized memories and the literary topoi of the *chansons de gestes* hardly form the soundest basis for an interpretation of the motives of Anglo-Norman conquerors. But the *chansons*, for all their exaggeration, reach parts of past societies which our conventional historical documentation – itself stylized in a form which we rarely recognize – scarcely penetrates. Nor is their testimony without occasional documentary support. Rarely could there be a more convincing example of the valiant knight riding to the rescue of the damsel in distress than that given in a prosaic contemporary chronicle recounting how Miles of Gloucester, future earl of Hereford (d. 1143), moved by 'the compassionate pity he felt for a noble woman', made a dangerous dash to rescue Richard fitz Gilbert's widow from Cardigan castle in 1136.[16] The sense of shared loyalty, adventure and enterprise of these men (almost Roland-and-Oliver-like in its intensity) occasionally surfaces in the evidence. It does so, for example, in Orderic's description of the

---

[13] *Song*, l. 1812; *Expugnatio*, pp. 36–7 (Bk 1, ch. 4); cf. pp. 49, 165.
[14] W. Dugdale, *Monasticon Anglicanum*, revised edn. ed. J. Caley *et al.* (6 vols. London, 1817–30), vol. vi, part i, pp. 349–50.
[15] *Itin. Kambrie*, pp. 89–90 (Bk 1, ch. 12); *Song*, ll. 1796–7.   [16] *Gesta Stephani*, pp. 18–19.

swashbuckling Robert of Rhuddlan being accompanied in his last desperate stand on the foreshore at Degannwy in north Wales (*c.* 1090) by his loyal knight, Osbern of Orgères, the very man who had earlier witnessed Robert's gifts to the Norman monastery of St Evroul; it does so again in the hard-headed business agreement of the 1190s – reminiscent of those of the Hundred Years' War – whereby Thomas de Verdun and Hugh de Lacy swore to share equally whatever they should win by conquest in Airgialla (Uriel).[17] Wales and Ireland until the end of the thirteenth century – and Ireland for long after – were military frontier societies where *chanson* and *geste*, life and legend – as in the Legend of Fulk Fitzwarin – easily met; that is all the more reason why we should not underestimate the impact of military values and ambitions in shaping the lives and aspirations of their conquerors.

The camaraderie shared by these conquering warriors is striking; but it was a camaraderie contained – as was that of Roland and Oliver – within the framework of lordship. That was the essential context of the movements which we call, by way of shorthand, the conquests of Wales and Ireland, as it was also of the Anglo-Norman penetration of Scotland. Such movements were informed by the basic principles of medieval aristocratic life, adventure and acquisitiveness, not by national animus nor by dreams of centralist regimentation nor by any necessary commitment to a co-ordinated plan. These aristocratic warriors took the world, including Wales and Ireland, as they found it; they adapted to it and exploited it to their own ends. They frequently chose brides from native society in order to ease their passage into, and domination of, it: Gerald of Windsor did so quite blatantly in Wales (as his grandson freely conceded); Hugh de Lacy, the first Anglo-Norman lord of Meath, furthered his ambitions in Ireland by taking a daughter of Ruaidrí Ó Conchobair (Rory O'Connor, king of Connacht (d. 1198)) as his second wife; while, to take a Scottish example, the earliest de Quincy to establish himself in Scotland quickly enhanced his prospects by taking a native heiress to wife. They worked with the grain of native society where it suited them: Hugh de Lacy, so we are told by Gerald, 'went to great trouble to conciliate those who had been conquered ... and enticed them to his side by his mild rule', while another of the early Anglo-Norman lords of Ireland, Raymond le Gros, showed his ecumenism by addressing one of his charters 'to all present and to come, French, English, Flemish, Welsh and Irish'.[18]

It was the commitment of these men which provided the essential momentum for the Anglo-Norman penetration into, and domination of, Wales, Ireland and, in a different form, Scotland. Their character, ambitions and

[17] Orderic Vitalis, *Historia Ecclesiastica*, vol. IV, p. 141; J. Mills and M. J. McEnery (eds.), *Calendar of the Gormanston Register* (Dublin, 1916), p. 144.
[18] *Expugnatio*, pp. 190–1 (Bk 2, ch. 21); E. St J. Brooks, 'An Unpublished Charter of Raymond le Gros', *Journal of the Royal Society of the Antiquaries of Ireland*, 7th series, 9 (1939), pp. 167–9.

policies substantially shaped the nature of that domination. The role of the English monarchy in the process was also crucial, as we shall see;[19] but given the monarchy's other commitments and ambitions, it was on the Anglo-Norman aristocracy – or rather that fairly small segment of it which took an active interest in the outlying parts of the British Isles – that most of the groundwork of conquest and domination devolved. This is obviously true in the first generation or so of Anglo-Norman penetration. Thus in Wales the pace and scope of the movement was largely determined by men such as Robert of Rhuddlan (d. *c.* 1088–93) in the north or Robert fitz Hamo (d. 1107) in Glamorgan, just as it was in Ireland a century later by aristocratic warriors such as the endlessly ambitious John de Courcy (d. *c.* 1219) or the remarkable William de Burgh (d. 1205–6) whose castles still 'convey an unmistakable impression of a forceful military mind verging on genius'.[20] But the centrality of aristocratic drive was almost as crucial in subsequent generations. Thus William Braose (d. 1211) seems to have breathed a new and terrible life into the Anglo-Norman penetration of central Wales in the late twelfth century, while it was the vigour and determination of Earl Gilbert 'the Red' of Gloucester (d. 1295) which finally brought the upland chieftains of Glamorgan under English control. In Ireland, likewise, individual magnates such as Earl Walter de Burgh (d. 1271) and his son Richard, the 'Red Earl' (d. 1326) or Thomas de Clare (d. 1287) set the stamp of their personalities and policies on the process of domination. Without this aristocratic commitment, the Anglo-Norman drive into Wales and Ireland quickly faltered, and ground was rapidly lost. That was why a prolonged minority or the succession of heiresses or a serious political miscalculation were so disastrous; they neutered the potency of an effectively aristocratic conquest or, rather, collection of conquests.

It was the aristocracy which provided the momentum for penetration into, and domination of, Wales, Ireland and in a different form Scotland. Within this aristocratic world the lord's household, his *familia* or *mesnie*, was the nodal point of enterprise and service, just as the king's household, especially his military household, was the motor of royal power.[21] Each household comprised a group of noisy and ambitious young men, bound by a lover-like devotion to their lord, a devotion kept fresh by the prospect of reward in pensions, loot or land. Earl Hugh the Fat of Chester (d. 1101), so it was said, 'was always surrounded by a huge household, full of the noise of swarms of

---

[19] Below ch. 4.

[20] C. A. Empey, 'The Settlement of the Kingdom of Limerick', in J. Lydon (ed.), *England and Ireland in the Later Middle Ages* (Dublin, 1981), p. 8.

[21] Cf. J. O. Prestwich, 'The Military Household of the Norman Kings', *English Historical Review*, 96 (1981), pp. 1–35. There is a striking analysis of an 'Anglo-Scottish' earl's *familia* by G. G. Simpson, 'The *Familia* of Roger de Quincy, Earl of Winchester and Constable of Scotland', in K. J. Stringer (ed.), *Essays on the Nobility of Medieval Scotland* (Edinburgh, 1985), pp. 102–30.

youths, of both noble and non-noble birth'.[22] Ties of service were frequently reinforced by ties of blood and marriage, both between the vassals themselves and between the vassals and their lord. This intertwining of marital, blood and service ties is particularly clear in the ranks of early *conquistadores* of Wales and Ireland. It was to his cousin, Robert 'of Tilleul' (later to be known as 'of Rhuddlan') that Earl Hugh of Chester entrusted the military command and conquest of his borderlands in north Wales, just as William fitz Osbern, earl of Hereford (d. 1071) placed his brother-in-law, Ralph de Tosny, in charge of one of the key routes into mid-Wales by granting him Clifford-on-Wye. In Ireland *The Song of Dermot and the Earl* vividly portrays the interplay (not always smooth) of marital and vassalage bonds in the careers of Robert de Quenci and Raymond le Gros, whose ties of vassalage, service and reward with Strongbow were reinforced by marrying into their lord's family.[23] Nowhere, of course, is the power of these twin ties of blood and service more effectively evoked than in Gerald of Wales' *Expugnatio Hibernica*, the family chronicle of an aggressive, tightly-knit and fiercely proud lay and ecclesiastical dynasty, the Geraldines, *Giraldide*.

It was from the ranks of his followers that the lord drew his manpower, especially in the early days of penetration. Lords readily acknowledged their debt to their followers in a touching fashion: William Braose (d. 1211) referred proudly to 'my men, dead and alive, who have served me faithfully and died in my cause', just as a Mortimer benefaction commemorated 'our men who died in the conquest of Maelienydd'.[24] The same sense of shared pride and adventure in the lord's service is reflected in a reference to those 'who first came to Ireland with Hugh de Lacy in his conquest (*ad conquestum suum*)'.[25] It was to these same men that the lord turned for advice in a predicament, as is vividly recounted of Strongbow in the *Song of Dermot and the Earl*; it was they who witnessed his most solemn grants, such as the gift to the abbey of St Thomas', Dublin guaranteed by 'the whole household' (*tota familia*) of Hugh de Lacy.[26] The lord, for his part, literally made his men, and nowhere more so than in his land of conquests. It was he who often built their castles for them in the first instance, since they would not have the wherewithal or power to do so; it was he who carved out an estate for them and granted it in return for immediate or prospective knight service; he also kept a close eye on them through his court and supervised and controlled their gifts and bequests.[27] The

22 Orderic Vitalis, *Historia Ecclesiasticas*, vol. III, p. 216.
23 *Song*, ll. 2741–50, 2828–60, 2994–3070.
24 W. Dugdale, *Monasticon Anglicanum*, vol. IV, p. 616; B. G. Charles, 'An Early Charter of the Abbey of Cwmhir', *Transactions of the Radnorshire Society*, 40 (1970), pp. 68–73.
25 *Chart. St Mary's, Dublin*, vol. I, p. 275.
26 *Song*, ll. 1798–1820; *Reg. St Thomas, Dublin*, 285.
27 *Expugnatio*, pp. 190–5 (Bk 2, ch. 21–ch. 23); G. H. Orpen, *Ireland under the Normans, 1169–1333* (4 vols., Oxford, 1911–20), vol. III, pp. 34–5; *Chart. St Mary's, Dublin*, vol. I, p. 45.

sense of mutual dependence between lord and follower was profound and sincere: William Marshal could speak with genuine affection of 'my most beloved and faithful knight' (*karissimus et fidelis miles meus*), William de St Leger; and the compliment could equally be returned, as in Adam de Feypo's grants in memory of his lord Hugh de Lacy.[28] Such bonds were, of course, basic in medieval society generally; but nowhere was their force greater or more intense than in military frontier societies such as Wales and Ireland. Indeed, precisely because the military situation in both countries remained precarious and unresolved for so long, the ties and obligations of feudal lordship and vassalage retained their *raison* and practical effectiveness long after they had begun to wither in England.

Given that conquest took place within the framework and under the guidance of lordship, the personality and drive of the individual lord was central to the success and tempo of conquest. Some of the *conquistadores* were political outcasts or *exclus* searching for the fortune and fame which might restore their careers, none more so than Richard fitz Gilbert, Strongbow (d. 1176), whose pedigree, in Gerald's memorable phrase, 'was longer than his purse'.[29] Others were men down on their luck, nursing chips on their shoulders and impatient of the constraints of royal policy. Some were illegitimates, such as Meiler fitz Henry, forced to make their own way in the world because of the taint in their blood; yet others – and in a way all of them – were men who could not resist the opportunity for a gamble or an adventure. Such was Arnulf of Montgomery who undertook the perilous task of establishing a Norman foothold in farthest Pembroke in the 1090s; such also was John de Courcy who undertook a similar task in Ulaid (Ulster) some eighty years later thereby becoming a legend in his own lifetime and doing more than a little to create and cultivate that legend. Arnulf of Montgomery and John de Courcy belong to another very distinctive category within the ranks of the invaders; they were both younger sons. They thus belonged to a group, the *juvenes*, which has attracted a good deal of attention of late from historians of the eleventh and twelfth centuries as at once one of the most enterprising and most disruptive forces in the history of the period. Some of them were young in years with all the carefree impetuousness such youthfulness implies: such was Roger Poer, 'a youth as yet unbearded, fair-haired, handsome and tall' who was one of de Courcy's lieutenants in Ulaid and who was to find an early grave in Ireland; such were the young sons of the Norman families of the Welsh March such as Clifford, Braose or Mortimer who were dispatched to the most dangerous frontier outposts or put in charge of border lordships to prove their mettle and staying power; such were the young men (*juveniles*) whose rashness

[28] *Reg. St Thomas, Dublin*, pp. 356–7; *Chart. St Mary's, Dublin*, vol. 1, p. 92.
[29] *Expugnatio* 54 (Bk 1, ch. 12); M.-T. Flanagan, 'Strongbow, Henry II and Anglo-Norman Intervention in Ireland', *War and Government in the Middle Ages. Essays in Honour of J. O. Prestwich*, eds. J. B. Gillingham and J. C. Holt (Woodbridge, 1984), pp. 62–77.

Robert Fitz Stephen and Miles de Cogan had difficulty in containing in south-west Ireland.[30] Many of these men were junior in the order of their birth as well as in years, and given the cult of primogeniture and lineage in feudal society they had to look for their fortunes other than from the patrimonial estates. So it was that Scotland became, in Professor Barrow's words, a land of opportunity for younger sons of Anglo-Norman families; so it was that a younger son, such as Adam of Hereford, hitched his wagon to the star of Strongbow and, when that wagon arrived at a gold-mine in Ireland, rushed home to Herefordshire to get his two elder brothers – with commendable fraternal love – to come to share in his luck.[31] The enterprise of younger sons was a crucial element well beyond the first generation or so of conquest. It was the second son of Hugh de Lacy (d. 1186), not the elder one, who maintained the momentum of Lacy expansion in Ireland; it was the cadet branches of Maurice fitz Gerald's descendants, rather than the senior branch, which proved to be the most enterprising; and it was Thomas de Clare (d. 1287), the virtually landless younger brother of the earl of Gloucester, who had the will and the appetite to take up the challenge of establishing English power in Thomond in the 1270s.

A few of these *conquistadores* showed that they did not have the stomach for their task: Philip Braose and Robert le Poer were both excoriated by Gerald of Wales for being lily-livered, while William Hautenot surrendered his border manor in Shropshire because, in an admission of unusual honesty, he was wearied with war.[32] But such weariness was exceptional. The Anglo-Norman barons who invaded Wales and Ireland were, by definition, men of large military appetites. They lived in a world habituated to violence.[33] They fought hard and often died violently – whether cut down by kings (as was William of Eu, lord of Caerleon, blinded and castrated by Rufus in 1096) or ambushed (as was the arrogant Richard fitz Gilbert of Clare in 1136 as he travelled through a wooded pass in Wales ostentatiously, and foolishly, preceded by a fiddler and a soloist!) or axed to death (as was Hugh de Lacy, the first Anglo-Norman lord of Meath, in 1186 as he was surveying one of his castles). What is difficult for the twentieth-century historical imagination is to capture their swaggering bravado and limitless ambition. They were indeed – as one of them was described – men 'of extreme arrogance and presumption'.[34] They took disaster in their stride: when Hugh de Lacy II (d. 1243) fell foul of King John in

[30] *Expugnatio*, pp. 177, 187 (Bk 2, ch. 17, ch. 30); Davies, *Conquest*, p. 85.

[31] Barrow, *Anglo-Norman Era*, ch. 1; *Reg. St Thomas, Dublin*, pp. 102–3.

[32] *Expugnatio*, pp. 178, 184–6, 190 (Bk 2, ch. 17, ch. 20, ch. 21); *Calendar of Inquisitions Post Mortem* (18 vols., London 1898–1988), vol. II, no. 747.

[33] Note, for example, the revealing phrase in one of the charters of Earl Roger of Hereford (d. 1155) – 'propter violentiam a rege vel ab aliquo potente', D. Walker (ed.), 'Charters of the Earldom of Hereford, 1095–1201', in *Camden Miscellany*, 22, Camden Society, 4th series, vol. 1 (London, 1964), p. 26.

[34] Howlett (ed.), *Chronicles of Stephen* etc., vol. IV, p. 184 (Hugh Mortimer).

1210, he fled to Scotland, found a new avenue for his military enterprise in the Albigensian crusade in southern France, fought hard to secure the recovery of his Irish lands which he achieved in 1227 and on his death could be commemorated as 'a most renowned warrior and the glorious conqueror of a great part of Ireland', just as his equally remarkable half-brother (the offspring of a union with an Irish woman) was hailed by an Irish annalist as 'chiefest champion in these parts of Europe, and the hardiest and strongest hand of any Englishman from the Nicene seas to this place'.[35] The two Lacy half-brothers may stand for the rest of these remarkable men. It would take the talents of a Prescott to describe their often larger-than-life qualities; but neither our modern sensitivities nor the conventions of modern academic historiography should surely conceal from us the obvious truism that their personalities (and those of some of their formidable womenfolk) were central to the process of conquest.

Such men did not work to a master-plan; nor did they defer to constitutional proprieties. They might seek the king's permission and approval, at least in a general fashion; but they were by instinct men of action who found it difficult to resist an opportunity for adventure or gain. For that reason we should treat with circumspection the explanations and justifications with which historians, medieval and modern, have surrounded their interventions. William the Conqueror, so medieval legend had it, had committed 'the lands of the March' of Wales to 'the most valiant knights of the host'.[36] So indeed he may have and no doubt he kept a watching brief over their activities; but in truth he did little more than license an instinct for aggression and expansion which he would have been the first to recognize. In Ireland, historians have naturally construc-ted their narratives around the pretexts for Anglo-Norman intervention provided in the contemporary sources – from the abduction of Derbforgaill (Dervorgilla) wife of the king of Bréifne in 1152 (the nearest that contemporary epic could get to Helen of Troy), *via* the papal bull *Laudabiliter* of 1155 (that notorious King Charles I's head of Irish historiography) and so eventually to the flight of Diarmait Mac Murchada to England in 1166 in search of support. The story is cogent, clear and contemporary; but it leaves unexplained why so many men eventually responded to the invitation. Equally, in the case of Scotland, we are constantly reminded of the policies of a modernizing monarchy as the essential background to the Anglo-Norman settlement of the twelfth and thirteenth centuries; but invitations have to be accepted. And they were. In other words it is among the Anglo-Norman warriors themselves that we should search for an explanation for their intervention.

That explanation should surely be simple. They saw an opportunity, as they

---

[35] Orpen, *Ireland under the Normans*, vol. III, pp. 255–6; Matthew Paris, *Chronica Majora*, vol. IV, p. 232; Annals of Clonmacnoise quoted in Otway-Ruthven, *Ireland*, p. 92.

[36] E. J. Hathaway *et al.* (eds.), *Fouke le Fitz Waryn*, Anglo-Norman Text Society (Oxford, 1975), p. 3.

did in countless other places in Europe or beyond; they grabbed it when the appropriate occasion arose; they rarely worked to a co-ordinated plan and there is, therefore, much that is spontaneous and piecemeal about their activities; they did not know where their enterprises might lead, and they would make the best they could of whatever situation they found themselves in – as did Strongbow when he even offered to hold Leinster as a vassal of Ruaidrí Ó Conchobair, king of Connacht, when he found himself in a tight spot.[37] Later Irish sources were not far wrong when they identified these men as suffering from an 'excess of rapacity' and for 'an eager lust for our lands'.[38] 'You were always pestering me for a portion of Wales', Henry I is alleged to have said to Gilbert fitz Richard of Clare (d. 1114–17), 'Now I will give you the land of Cadwgan ap Bleddyn. Go and take possession of it'.[39] The conversation is imaginary, but it is at least informed by contemporary imagination, and surely takes us closer to the world of the conquerors than do the land charters. It is echoed in *The Song's* comment that Henry II granted Ulster to John de Courcy, 'if he could conquer it by force'.[40] Even in Scotland, one suspects – one can do no more – that some of the grants of the Scottish kings to Anglo-Norman barons were a response to approaches and appeals.[41]

Native rulers learnt quickly how to pander to the greed of these upwardly mobile Anglo-Normans. They issued prospectuses which appealed to their natural acquisitiveness. Here again the literary sources speak at least with the conviction of contemporary imagination, as in the prospector's charter which *The Song* puts in King Diarmait's mouth: 'Whoever shall wish for land or pence, / Horses, armour or chargers, / Gold or silver, I shall give them very ample pay. Whoever shall wish / for soil or sod, / Richly shall I enfeoff them.'[42] I used the metaphor of the market to describe the character of these men, and I used it deliberately. They were inveterate gamblers on a bull market. Nowhere was that more obvious than in their dabbling in futures. They spoke of their 'future acquisitions' and made grants from them; they secured licences to hold any lands which they might in future conquer from the Welsh or Irish as additions to their existing baronies.[43] They secured speculative grants of land if only to stake out a pre-emptive claim, as in the grant of the whole or part of Connacht to William de Burgh in the 1190s.[44] Kings were willing to make such

[37] *Song*, ll. 1835–6.
[38] *Caithréim* (as cited above, ch. 1, n. 34), vol. II, p. 2; E. Curtis and R. B. McDowell (eds.), *Irish Historical Documents 1172–1922* (London, 1943), p. 43 (Remonstrance of 1317).
[39] *Brut*, p. 34.   [40] *Song*, ll. 2733–4.
[41] Cf. Duncan, *Scotland*, p. 137 ('or even to seek').
[42] *Song*, ll. 431–6.
[43] 'Cartulary of Brecon Priory', *Archaeologia Cambrensis*, 4th series, vol. XIV (1883), p. 148; J. Conway Davies (ed.), *Episcopal Acts and Cognate Documents relating to Welsh Dioceses 1066–1272*, Historical Society of the Church in Wales (2 vols. Cardiff, 1946–8), vol. II, p. 644; *Rotuli Chartarum in Turri Londinensi asservati, 1199–1216* (London, 1837), vol. I, part I, p. 66; *Calendar of Patent Rolls 1258–66*, p. 674.
[44] Orpen, *Ireland under the Normans*, vol. II, p. 156.

grants, partly to give a head to restless and importuning nobles, partly to ease the pressures on their patronage resources elsewhere, partly to encourage effort, and partly to secure a temporary alliance or support in return for an unrealistic and unrealisable future reward (of which there can be no more blatant example than the grant by King John of much of north-east Ireland to Alan fitz Roland of Galloway for the service of 140 knights in 1212).[45] The stakes these men played for were massive, proportionately as massive as the 'empires' of the Norman and Angevin rulers themselves: the whole of Glamorgan and Gwynllŵg; the old Welsh kingdom of Brycheiniog (Brecon); the provincial kingdom of Meath 'as Murchad Ua Máel Sechlainn (Murrough O'Melaghlin, d. 1153) or any one else before or after him most fully held it';[46] or the five and half cantreds in Limerick which was Theobald Walter's original endowment in 1185; the whole of Annandale to Robert Brus in 1124; or Cunningham and most of Lauderdale to Hugh de Morville. We have, perhaps, not stood sufficiently in awe of the scale of these grants. Annandale extended over 200,000 acres, while the lands given to Theobald Walter embraced some half a million statute acres.[47] These were, at least prospectively, vast regional supremacies and they came, whether explicitly (as in the case of Meath) or implicitly, with many of the powers of native lordship or kingship attached to them. It is little wonder that with such fortunes to be made this was a gambler's paradise. We get an authentic whiff of its atmosphere in the grant to Philip de Barry, Gerald of Wales' brother, of two cantreds in the kingdom of Cork which should fall to him 'by lot'.[48] Equally it comes as no surprise that some gamblers gambled beyond their means: not the least of the reasons that King John was able to destroy William de Braose so completely and with a veneer of legality was that he was able to foreclose on the massive proffer of 5,000 marks which William had made for the honour of Limerick in January 1201.

Prospective grants and future acquisitions could only be converted into realizable assets through immense effort and, above all, with the support of devoted followers. Those followers in turn expected a share of the winnings. Indeed military strategy, effective territorial domination and an ethos of obligatory aristocratic largess all dictated that they should partake in their lord's good fortune. 'He was not merely generous, but prodigal', was the compliment paid to Earl Hugh of Chester.[49] He and his like had much to be prodigal with – booty, plunder, ransoms and above all land. The prospects for the followers of these men were truly dazzling. Many of the grants they

---

[45] *CDI*, vol. I, nos. 427, 468.   [46] *Calendar of the Gormanston Register*, p. 177.

[47] These estimates are, respectively those of Barrow, *Kingship and Unity*, p. 32 and C. A. Empey, 'The Norman period, 1185–1500', in W. Nolan (ed.), *Tipperary: History and Society. Interdisciplinary Essays on the History of an Irish county* (Dublin, 1985), 78.

[48] Quoted in Orpen, *Ireland under the Normans*, vol. II, p. 43 ('duas alias cantredas in regno Corchaiae prout sorte obvenient ei').

[49] Orderic Vitalis, *Historia Ecclesiastica*, vol. II, p. 260.

received were, indeed, initially themselves prospective, more in the nature of military commands (at least in parts of Ireland and Wales) which could only be converted into profitable territorial lordship by strenuous effort. Such no doubt were the grants that Gilbert fitz Richard of Clare made to his followers in Ceredigion in the early twelfth century or Strongbow to his followers in Leinster in the 1170s (of which the grant of the half cantred of Aghaboe to Adam of Hereford is an early example).[50] Nevertheless as the opportunities for territorial scoops and major changes to the landed order became increasingly restricted in England, so the prospect of making a fortune elsewhere in the British Isles grew the more attractive. The circle of acquisitiveness was thereby enlarged in a succession of related ripples. It is here surely – obvious truism that it may sound – that we must locate the momentum of the Anglo-Norman domination of the British Isles; the ambitions of Scottish monarchs or the invitations of Irish king or the raids of Welsh princes provided no more than pretexts and opportunities.

Ambition was a close twin to acquisitiveness in the make-up of these men. Orderic Vitalis had diagnosed the Norman condition shrewdly: they were, he remarked, 'a warlike race ... moved by fierce ambition to lord it over others' and, one might add, anxious not to be subject to too demanding a lordship themselves.[51] It is difficult not to believe that part of the attraction of Wales, Scotland and Ireland for at least some of these men was that they provided them with an opportunity to flex the muscles of their ambitions and pretensions rather more freely and arrogantly than in an England dominated by royal power and presence. By the thirteenth century in Wales they were beginning to clothe their pretensions in the respectable guise of 'Marcher liberties' and claiming that those liberties – *iura regalia* as they called them – were based on 'ancient conquest'.[52] But beneath the quasi-judicial language lay the arrogance of independence. William Braose lifted the curtain on it when he remarked defiantly in 1199 that 'neither the king nor the justiciar nor the sheriff ought to interfere in his liberty'. The methods of another Welsh marcher lord, Walter Clifford (d. 1263), were even more direct: when he received a royal message that was not to his liking, he made the messenger eat his words literally – parchment, seal and all. John fitz Alan of Oswestry and Clun (d. 1272) was equally impudent, albeit in words not in actions; he blurted out impetuously that 'in the parts of the March ... he was obliged to do nothing at the king's mandate and nothing would he do'.[53] The date and

50 J. G. Edwards, 'The Normans and the Welsh March', *Proceedings of the British Academy* 42 (1956), pp. 155–77; E. Curtis (ed.), *Calendar of Ormond Deeds 1172–1603*, Irish Manuscripts Commission (6 vols., Dublin, 1932–43), vol. I, p. 1; Cunningham, *Anglo-Norman Advance* (as cited above, ch. 1, n. 26), pp. 59–61, 159–61.

51 Orderic Vitalis, *Historia Ecclesiastica*, vol. V, p. 24.

52 R. R. Davies, 'Kings, Lords and Liberties in the March of Wales 1066–1272', *Transactions Royal Historical Society*, 5th series, 29 (1979), pp. 41–61.

53 Quoted in Davies, *Lordship and Society in the March of Wales*, pp. 1, 218.

circumstances of the Anglo-Norman intervention in Ireland and some sharp raps over the knuckles by Henry II and John taught the Anglo-Norman lords there to moderate their language and their claims. Nevertheless they enjoyed playing the rôle of petty kings, even to the extent, in John de Courcy's case, of issuing their own coins without the king of England's name on them, formulating their own military policies, waging 'private' wars on each other as well as on the king, and playing at making and unmaking kings among the native Irish. It is little wonder that the kings of England suffered bouts of paranoia about Anglo-Norman lords in Wales and Ireland. The situation was, of course, different in Scotland: it was a kingdom in its own right and the Anglo-Norman settler families were deeply beholden to the royal dynasty for their promotion. Even there, the growth of a Stewart power-base radiating from Bute and Kintyre meant that by the late-thirteenth century 'the Stewarts were among the most powerful of West Highland chiefs, disposing of a sizeable fleet of galleys and commanding the loyalty of a large number of Gaelic-speaking tenants and dependants'.[54] It was the thrusting ambition of such men – an ambition which worked to no set plan but equally knew no limits other than those of its own power – which lay at the heart of the process of domination throughout the British Isles. It is little wonder that contemporaries, native and Anglo-Norman alike, thought that such men aspired to kingship and that a few of them should have attained it. Thus it was as 'king of Meath' that Hugh de Lacy was memorialized by an Irish annalist, while Roger of Howden (intimate of the English royal court that he was) felt it appropriate to refer to John de Courcy as 'prince of the kingdom of Ulster in Ireland'.[55]

To men of such brazen and congenital acquisitiveness, domination was secured by methods most suited to their talents and commensurate with their needs and ambitions. They might well have adopted as their motto the phrase applied, albeit in a different context, by a Domesday commissioner to one of the Norman lords of the Welsh frontier: 'He has there what he can take; nothing else.'[56] As warriors it was to the sword that they reached most readily to claim and assert their domination; and it was a title 'by ancient conquest' which was, therefore, the natural basis of their claims in subsequent generations. As an Irish poet was to put it swaggeringly, 'The charter of the sword: what better one is there?'[57] The sword of the Anglo-Normans was a particularly sharp and effective one. There can be little doubt that the initial overwhelming impact of Anglo-Norman invaders on Wales and Ireland represented the victory of superior military technology and tactics – notably,

[54] Barrow, *Anglo-Norman Era*, pp. 69–70.
[55] W. M. Hennessy (ed.), *Annals of Loch Cé*, Rolls Series (2 vols., London, 1871), vol. I, p. 173; Roger Howden quoted in R. Frame, *Colonial Ireland, 1169–1369* (Dublin, 1981), p. 28.
[56] V. H. Galbraith (ed.), *The Herefordshire Domesday*, Pipe Roll Society, new series, 25 (London, 1950), p. 65.
[57] Quoted in J. F. Lydon, 'The Problem of the Frontier in Medieval Ireland', *Topic. A Journal of the Liberal Arts* (Washington, Pennsylvania), 13 (1967), p. 19.

of course, heavily armed cavalry, carefully deployed bands of archers, and the rapidly-built castle.[58]

The initial shock tactic was the harrying expedition. Its character is vividly evoked in several contemporary native descriptions such as this one: 'A mighty hosting this year [1201] in Desmond by William [de Burgh] and other foreigners ... Their plundering parties were sent ... and committed great depredations ... They spent a week there and made great raids and burnt crops in every place they came to.'[59] The aim of such harryings, very much like the *chevauchées* of English armies in fourteenth-century France, was painfully obvious. It was *vastatio*, the deliberate destruction of the resources of the people to be subjected and thereby of the authority and credibility of its rulers. There was also a profiteering element: plunder was collected in large, sometimes unmanageable, quantities, whether by way of spoils or by way of fines to buy off further depredations. Such plundering was regarded as having a low risk and a high profit element;[60] contemporary sources in Wales and Ireland make it clear that it was regarded as a regular and important aspect of Anglo-Norman activity and raids. It helped to provide stores and replenish provisions for hard-pressed armies; it was also a crucial way of restoring morale to underpaid and disaffected troops. But harrying also had a more calculatingly 'political' dimension: its aim was to intimidate the opposing forces to the negotiating table, or in contemporary language to come to parley, give hostages, and make peace on the invader's terms.[61] In other words, the harrying raid was often the essential prelude to domination or at least to a qualified surrender.

The instrument and symbol *par excellence* of that domination was, of course, the castle. That was the case throughout Europe in the eleventh and twelfth centuries. It was a continent where domination, power and aggression revolved very considerably around the castle and the castle-owners. As it was said of one French lord, he could do what he liked without fear, since he could rely on the protection of his castle, whereas his peers and neighbours did not own a castle.[62] Castle owners, therefore, were the true *potentes*. Initially a

---

[58] R. Bartlett, 'Technique militaire et pouvoir politique, 900–1300', *Annales, Economies, Sociétés, Civilisations*, 41 (1986), pp. 1138–59. There are striking contemporary Welsh descriptions of Anglo-Norman military tactics as seen through native eyes in *Brut*, pp. 42–4; D. Simon Evans (ed.), *Historia Gruffud Vab Kenan* (Cardiff, 1977), p. 26.

[59] S. Mac Airt (ed.), *The Annals of Inisfallen* (Dublin, 1951), p. 329.

[60] Note, for example, the annalist's comment – 'These expeditions were profitable to the Galls, who got much booty thereby, though not incurring the dangers of the conflict', A. Martin Freeman (ed.), *The Annals of Connacht* (Dublin, 1944), p. 17.

[61] *Song*, ll. 2777–82: 'The earl entered Offaly / with all his chivalry / In order to spoil and plunder / O'Dempsey, who was so bold, / In that he did not deign to parley with the earl / Nor would deliver hostages to him.' For excellent discussions of the nature of Irish and Anglo-Irish warfare see K. Simms, 'Warfare in the medieval Gaelic lordships', *Irish Sword*, 12 (1975), 98–108, and R. Frame, 'War and Peace in the Medieval Lordship of Ireland', in J. Lydon (ed.), *The English in Medieval Ireland* (Dublin, 1984), 118–41.

[62] Quoted in Jean Dunbabbin, *France in the Making 843–1180* (Oxford, 1985), p. 146.

castle may have done no more than stake out an advance military claim, as in the forward castles hurriedly thrown up by the Anglo-Normans in north-west Wales in the 1090s. But so rapid and apparently inexorable was the Anglo-Norman advance that the castle quickly became – or could become – a symbol of domination rather than merely a military outpost. Nowhere was that more obviously so than in Wales, Ireland and Scotland where the castle was the visible sign of a new dispensation and a foreign lordship. In the phrase of *The Song of Dermot and the Earl*, it literally rooted the new lords in their conquered lands.[63] Building a castle was regarded as a *sine qua non* of new lordship; failure to do so could incur the threat of confiscation.[64] A crash-campaign of castle building was undertaken, generally under the direction and at the expense of a great lord, such as William fitz Osbern or Hugh de Lacy, or of the king as in the case of Henry II on his visit to Ireland in 1171–2, but amply supported, especially in the second generation, by their vassals. The results are quite staggering, especially if viewed as a whole. During the century or so before 1215 parts of Wales, Scotland and Ireland came to bristle with a remarkable number of mottes and ringworks – such as the ninety-four (at the latest count) built in Meath, the twenty mottes and unknown number of ringworks which dominated the midland corridor from Durrow to Thurles, the great concentration of twenty-seven castles which controlled the strategic Vale of Montgomery on the Welsh border, or the thick clusters of mottes in the Clyde valley, Ayrshire and the valleys running down to the Solway Firth in Scotland.[65]

The crucial rôle of these castles in establishing Anglo-Norman domination (in the fullest sense of that word) was recurrently recognized by contemporaries; it extended much further than military power and further than historians have sometimes been willing to recognize. Born in violence, the castle was seen as an instrument for bringing order, peace and stability. It converted conquest and raid into domination and lordship: 'Earl Hugh of Chester', commented a Welsh biographer, 'made castles and fortified places according to the custom of the French and became lord of the land.'[66] Gerald of Wales' description of the purpose and achievement of Hugh de Lacy's great castle-building enterprise in Leinster and Meath echoes the same assumption: 'when (the Irish) had been hemmed in by castles and gradually subdued, (Hugh) compelled them to obey the laws'.[67] Furthermore the power of the castle was seen as the essential prerequisite for the effectiveness of lordship; it

---

[63] *Song*, ll. 3203–7.   [64] *Reg. St Thomas, Dublin*, pp. 43, 205–6, 211; *CDI*, vol. i, no. 913.

[65] *NHI*, vol. ii, pp. 214–16; B. J. Graham, 'The Mottes of the Norman Liberty of Meath' in H. Murtagh (ed.), *Irish Midland Studies* (Athlone, 1980), pp. 39–86; Cunningham, *Anglo-Norman Advance*, p. 172; D. J. Cathcart King and C. J. Spurgeon, 'The Mottes in the Vale of Montgomery', *Archaeologia Cambrensis*, 114 (1964–5), pp. 69–87; G. G. Simpson and B. Webster, 'Charter Evidence and the Distribution of Mottes in Scotland' in Stringer (ed.), *Nobility of Medieval Scotland*, pp. 1–13.

[66] *Historia Gruffud vab Kenan*, p. 18.   [67] *Expugnatio*, p. 190 (Bk 2, ch. 21).

was at once the emblem and guarantor of domination. This equation of castle and domination recurs, often sub-consciously, in the documentation of the period: the castle, so it is said, is the headquarters of the land (*caput terrae*); it was from the castle that the new lordship very frequently took its name; indeed the lordship was seen as being appurtenant to the castle (*dominium castri de X*), for, as a later survey of a Welsh castle put it eloquently, the castle 'is the common focus for the whole lordship, for it is to this castle that the whole lordship is dependent, intendent and annexed as its principal seat'. It was the jurisdictional, governmental and fiscal seat of lordship, the civilian as well as the military source of domination.[68]

The castle had one other function; it was the focus of settlement. The relationship between castle-building and alien colonization is again a recurrent one in the documentation of the period. Thus when William Rufus wished to make it abundantly clear that Cumberland lay within his kingdom, not within that of the king of Scots, he brought into the district foreign knights to garrison the castle he built at Carlisle and 'sent very many peasants thither with their wives and live-stock to settle there and till the soil'.[69] Much in the same fashion Gilbert fitz Richard of Clare imported English settlers to colonize Ceredigion once he and his henchmen had secured their control of the region by a process of incastellation; while, to give an Irish example, Philip de Barry specifically gave land in a grant 'which is so close to my castle that it can be easily and conveniently cultivated from the said castle'.[70] This close relationship between castle and colonization is also suggestively supported by archaeological evidence. Thus recent work on the motte at Kells (co. Kilkenny) has indicated that its purpose from its earliest days was as a centre of domination as much as of defence and that it quickly became 'a focus of non-military settlement' and for intensive economic exploitation. Recent studies of the castellation of Munster, notably the areas around Thurles and Roscrea, also suggest how closely castle-building, settlement and economic exploitation went hand in hand.[71] The formula was also one which operated in reverse. When a great revolt swept Galloway in 1174 an English chronicler reported that not only were all the castles destroyed but also that all the English and 'French' were slain; likewise when a Welsh princeling demolished the castles of Gower in 1217 he also 'drove all the English away from that land and took from them their chattels ... and he divided their lands for Welshmen to occupy'.[72]

Settlement was, of course, an accessory to domination; it underpinned and

68 Davies, 'Kings, Lords and Liberties', 47–8.
69 G. N. Garmonsway (ed.), *The Anglo-Saxon Chronicle* (London, 1953), p. 227.
70 *Reg. St Thomas, Dublin*, p. 214.
71 T. B. Barry, E. Culleton and C. A. Empey, 'Kells Motte, county Kilkenny', *Proceedings of the Royal Irish Academy*, 84 (1984) Section C, pp. 157–70; Cunningham, *The Norman Advance*, pp. 74–6.
72 Stubbs (ed.), *Gesta Regis Henrici Secundi* (as cited above, ch. 1, n. 40), vol. 1, pp. 67–8; *Brut*, p. 96.

secured that domination. Colonization, it is true, was often highly localized, confined to a few well-chosen districts where land was good, opportunities attractive, and the necessary security feasible. Such colonization owed as much to the demographic imperatives of a rising population and overcrowded villages – as the Flemish settlements in England, Scotland and Wales make clear – as to aristocratic inducements and policies. Indeed in some areas, such as lowland Glamorgan, the colonization movement from England may well have got under way before the Anglo-Norman lords invaded the country. Nevertheless, as so often in medieval society, colonization and settlement 'took place within the controlling framework of lordship'.[73] The Normans may have come to Wales and Ireland – as they had to England – as warrior lords; but their eyes were fixed on the regular income of domination as well as on the short-term pillage of victory. Entrepreneurship, after all, is only the acceptable face of acquisitiveness; and ruthlessly acquisitive the Anglo-Normans and their followers most certainly were. In Wales and Ireland they quickly seized – and created – opportunities to entrench their position and maximize their profits – founding boroughs and reserving land specifically for the purpose, creating manorial demesnes, exploiting the arable and pastoral resources of their new lordships, building mills, and inviting colonists (even possibly compelling them) to come to settle and offering them favourable and attractive terms for doing so.[74] Most of this dramatic story of economic domination and exploitation is hidden from us, at least until the thirteenth century when the evidence begins to become more abundant; but it is clear that it parallels in almost every respect a similar saga of domination, colonization and exploitation which was taking place in other peripheral areas of Europe – notably beyond the Elbe, in Spain and even in the Latin kingdom of Jerusalem. What also needs to be emphasized is that the movement from military supremacy to economic exploitation and colonization – though it could be long-drawn-out – often took place within a remarkably short period. The caravans of the settlers were arriving in the castle bailey on the morrow of the imposition of military domination. Thus already in 1086, within a few years of the Norman penetration of north-east Wales, the districts along the Dee estuary were being colonized (or recolonized); Norman lordship and control was everywhere evident. Much the same was true in Ireland a century later: the enterprise of the Anglo-Norman lords such as Hugh Lacy at Drogheda or William Marshal at New Ross reveals their keen eye for commercial opportunities, as does King John's directive to his justiciar in 1204 that he 'select for the king's use the two thirds of Connacht in which the best towns

[73] Frame, *Colonial Ireland*, p. 70.
[74] See especially, for Ireland, C. A. Empey, 'Conquest and Settlement: Patterns of Anglo-Norman Settlement in North Munster and South Leinster', *Irish Economic and Social History* 13 (1986), pp. 5–31, and B. J. Graham, *Anglo-Norman Settlement in Ireland*, Irish Settlement Studies (Athlone, 1985).

and harbours lie . . . and should found towns and assess rents in those parts'.[75] The first surviving Irish Pipe Roll of 1211–12 likewise shows how quickly and thoroughly the new lords set about exploiting the arable and pastoral wealth of eastern and southern Ireland.

Domination was, therefore, the prelude to settlement and exploitation, and to the exercise of the managerial and entrepreneurial qualities which, it has been claimed, characterized Anglo-Norman lordship, especially by the later twelfth century. But it cannot be emphasized too strongly that the forms of Anglo-Norman domination within the outlying countries of the British Isles varied immensely from place to place – from direct rule, intensive exploitation and considerable colonization on the one hand to a loose overlordship and the collection of tributary renders on the other. Two factors in particular determined the form that domination would take: on the one hand were the ambitions of the *conquistadores*, their numbers, and their calculation of how quickly they could convert their domination into a secure, well-entrenched and profitable lordship; on the other hand was the nature of the society which they were seeking to dominate, the character of political power and economic exploitation within it, and the attractiveness or otherwise of the district to be dominated. As in so many other directions, the Anglo-Normans proved infinitely adaptable, adjusting the forms of their authority to what was feasible. Thus, at Monmouth by 1086 the Norman lord, William fitz Baderon, had established his knights and they had seven ploughs there; but from the Welsh he collected tributes in honey, pigs and sheep as had been the custom of the Welsh princes.[76] The two forms of lordship and exploitation co-existed; the purpose of both was to augment the power and income of the Anglo-Normans. The nature of lordship varied greatly within England itself, especially as between southern and northern, lowland and highland, England; but rarely were the contrasts so sharp as in the outlying districts of the British Isles which fell under Anglo-Norman control.

It was not only the forms of domination and exploitation which differed from place to place; so did the forms of penetration. The Anglo-Normans were, of course, not afraid of bludgeoning would-be subjects into submission; but equally they were quite content to use less brutal methods, where they worked. Thus in much of Gwent, Glamorgan and Cemais in Wales or in south-west and north-east Munster and west Meath in Ireland, for example, Anglo-Norman penetration appears to have been relatively peaceful, albeit that military power lay not too far in the background. The Anglo-Normans often made their initial entry by invitation (as in Gwent, Scotland and Leinster); but they were the sort of guests who once invited had no intention of leaving. The opportunity *par excellence* for the Anglo-Normans to make a relatively peaceful entry lay, of course, in the deep fissures and internecine

---

[75] *CDI*, vol. I, no. 222.   [76] *Domesday Book* (4 vols., London 1783–1816), vol. I, f. 180 b.

feuds of native dynasties. It could even happen in Scotland: when Alexander I (1107–24) seemed reluctant to confirm lands in the south of the country to his young brother David, he was quickly brought to his senses by the threat that David might invite a force of Normans to come to help him to establish his claim. That, of course, is what happened recurrently in, and between, the fragmentary polities of native Wales and Ireland. Thus it was in the service of Caradog ap Gruffudd (d. 1081), in his struggle with a fellow member of his dynasty, Maredudd ab Owain (d. 1072), that the Normans made their initial entrée into Gwent in the 1070s; while Murchad, son of Ruaidrí Ó Conchobair, invited them in 1177 'to destroy Connacht, for evil towards his father'.[77] The Anglo-Normans, of course, did more than join in the fun; they exploited it ruthlessly to their own ends. They were brazen about their intentions. Gifts were deliberately given 'so that dissension may be moved between families', or, as the *Caithréim* said of Thomas de Clare, 'he resolved to nourish the . . . schism (within the Ó Briain dynasty) until such time as, they and their vassal chiefs being enfeebled mutually, he might step in and filch the country from them both'.[78] Promises were made to pretenders 'to exalt them over and above their kinsmen', while ousted segments had their expectations of getting their due share of the family lands raised on promise of practical displays of loyalty.[79] Nowhere, perhaps, is the *Realpolitik* of the invaders better captured than in the doubtless imaginary, but utterly convincing, interview that the justiciar of Ireland is alleged to have had with Edward I in 1278. When the king expressed concern at the anarchy that was Irish politics, the justiciar replied suavely that 'in policie he thought it expedient to winke at one knave cutting off another, and that would save the king's coffers and purchase peace to the land; whereat the king smiled and bid him return to Ireland'.[80] There was nothing that the most cynical and double-dealing of modern operators could have taught these men.

Once entrenched they exercised their domination in ways which best conformed with the realities of power. In large parts of Wales and Ireland that meant that they were often content with the exercise of overlordship. Native rulers were frequently left undisturbed so long as they acknowledged some degree of subjection. Formal relationships, lubricated by gifts, visits and subsidies, were entered into. Submissions were made, and tributes and services paid, as they had indeed been paid to native overkings of old. Indeed what we often call Anglo-Norman domination was the displacement of a native overlordship, more or less exacting and effective, by an alien overlordship,

[77] Quoted in Orpen, *Ireland under the Normans*, vol. II, p. 26.
[78] *Calendar of the Justiciary Rolls of Ireland 1295–1307* (2 vols., Dublin, 1905–14), vol. II, p. 354; *Caithréim*, vol. II, p. 10.
[79] *Brut*, pp. 29, 38, 40–1.
[80] Quoted from Hanmer's Chronicle in Orpen, *Ireland under the Normans*, vol. IV, pp. 109–10.

equally more or less exacting and effective.[81] The Annals of Loch Cé put the point vividly in its obituary of Hugh de Lacy, one of the earliest and most powerful of the Anglo-Norman lords of Ireland, on his death in 1186: 'he was king of Midhe and Breifne and Airghaill and it was to him that the tribute of Connacht was paid'.[82] The native chronicler was not in doubt that Hugh de Lacy exercised a domination commensurate with that of an Irish king and on terms comprehensible in Irish society. Elsewhere in his Irish lordship, especially in eastern Meath, Hugh's lordship over manors and knightly vassals was a domination perfectly comprehensible in terms of the pattern of seignorial authority in contemporary England. The two forms of authority were complementary; they reflected the differing situations which the Anglo-Normans confronted in different parts of Wales and Ireland and their different responses to them. Conquest was not uniform in its results or exclusively military in its methods. As in many other societies in different parts of the world, the radius and character of external domination extended from the intensive and authoritative on the one hand to the diffused and occasional on the other. But by whatever routes they reached it, what the Anglo-Norman lords wanted was domination. And that, to a greater or lesser degree and in varying forms, they had secured over much of Wales and Ireland by 1250 and, though acquired in a different form, over much of Scotland also.

[81] Cf. K. Simms, 'The Medieval Kingdom of Lough Erne', *Clogher Record*, 9 (1977), 130.
[82] *Annals of Loch Cé*, vol. I, p. 173.

3

Native submission

Domination was frequently founded on the brutal reality of military might. The Anglo-Normans were never slow to use the sword to gain, assert and retain mastery. They were in no way embarrassed in referring to what they had achieved in Wales and Ireland as a 'conquest'.[1] On the contrary they beatified the memory of the original pioneers, referring to them proudly as 'conqueror' and 'the first conqueror' and glorying in their conquering enterprises.[2] Military men, after all, are unlikely to have reservations about the militarism of their victories or to be slow to announce them to the world as such. Furthermore, the character of the Anglo-Norman penetration of Wales and Ireland – punctuated as it was by frequent reverses and recurrent massacres – helped to ensconce the terminology and presuppositions of enmity and confrontation deep in the consciousness of the period and thereby, through refraction, in historical writing on the period. Scotland was, of course, different; but the speed with which a terminology and mythology of abuse were developed from the mid 1290s by both Scots and English – most memorably epitomized in the comment attributed to Edward I in 1296 as he handed over the great seal of Scotland: 'A man does good business when he rids himself of a turd'[3] – shows how rapidly the language and stance of confrontation could likewise be adopted there.

Yet such a ready surrender to contemporary concepts of conquest and confrontation, and to the hindsight which informs them, may not always serve us well in our attempt to characterize the relationship between the Anglo-Normans and the political societies of Ireland, Scotland and Wales. Subjection was not always yielded, or demanded, at the point of the sword. It not infrequently took the form of willing and, indeed, optimistic surrender. Relationships between natives and newcomers were not infrequently cordial, even if some of the cordiality was contrived or forced. The Normans often

---

[1] For example, *Cal. Ormond Deeds* (as cited above, ch. 2, n. 50) vol. 1, pp. 364–5; *Close Rolls 1241–7*, pp. 348–9; *1251–3*, p. 458; *1254–6*, p. 413; *CDI*, vol. 11, no. 1482.
[2] *Chart. St Mary's Dublin*, vol. 1, pp. 275, 530; *Cal. Justiciary Rolls of Ireland*, vol. 1, pp. 281–2; Davies, *Lordship and Society*, p. 68.
[3] Quoted in Barrow, *Bruce*, p. 61.

made their *entrée* as allies and by invitation. It was so in Gwynedd and Gwent; it was so in Scotland; and it was so in Leinster, where Gerald of Wales had the good grace to call Diarmait Mac Murchada 'our excellent and generous benefactor'.[4] Even when submission was exacted after a military showdown, or at least the threat of one, the relationship between lord and dependant was not infrequently construed – albeit rather optimistically – as one of mutual friendship rather than one of grovelling surrender. Thus when Ruaidrí Ó Conchobair, king of Connacht, came to terms with Henry II in 1175 the diplomatic form of their agreement was that of a final concord, a bargain between equals; and likewise, when four years earlier Henry concluded an agreement with the Lord Rhys of Deheubarth, the native Welsh chronicler saw it, perhaps understandably, as the restoration of friendship as much as a submission.[5] In our rather legalistic, indeed sometimes anachronistic, scrutiny of the terminology of dependence and in a rather Whiggish anxiety to plot submissions on a graph of the inevitable intensification of lordship, we are perhaps in danger of losing sight of the element of reciprocal dependence and friendship, *amicitia*, and of the establishment of a formal relationship which might be involved in such submissions.

For the same reason we often approach genuine professions of the ready acceptance of overlordship with undue cynicism. When Fedlimid Ó Conchobair (Felim O'Connor), king of Connacht 1230–65, protested that 'for no promise made to him by the Irish had he receded or would recede from the king's service; he placed himself, his people and all he had under the protection of the king and the Lord Edward', or when Domnall Ruad Mac Carthaig (Donald Rufus MacCarthy) of Desmond maintained that he 'vehemently desired to be subjected to the king's domination and wished beyond measure to acquire the king's friendship by his service', we should take such statements at their face value, regardless of what motives we may believe lay behind them.[6] These men and many like them could hardly wait to make their submissions and professions of loyalty so that they could bask in the sun of their overlord's favour and support.

Nor were English kings and lords necessarily insensitive when confronted with such approaches. They knew full well that pandering to a vassal's sense of self-importance and boosting his morale were among the essential arts of lordship, 'good lordship' as it would be called in later generations. Henry I was a master of those arts: when he wanted to secure the submission of Owain ap Cadwgan of Powys (d. 1116), the most mercurial and daredevil Welsh princeling of his day, he 'joyfully received him . . . and did him honour and praised him'.[7] One can almost hear Owain purring with satisfaction as he was

4 *Expugnatio*, pp. 48–9 (Bk 1, ch. 9).
5 Roger of Howden, *Chronica*, ed. W. Stubbs, Rolls Series (4 vols., London, 1868–71) vol. II, p. 84; *Brut*, p. 66.
6 *CDI*, vol. II, nos. 713, 2362.   7 *Brut*, p. 38.

fondly stroked by such a munificent patron. So were submissions secured. Cajolery, persuasion and affability were necessary lubricants in the process. Even King John, hardly a noted exponent of such qualities, could on occasion try to display them. While on the borders of Wales in July 1216 he dispatched a letter to some leading Welshmen as follows: 'Know that we are coming to these parts for your convenience and not to harm or diminish you, as you will soon recognize from our actions. Please come to our faith and service as soon and as safely as you can; if you do so, you can rest assured that we will in no way diminish you but will maintain and protect you and yours as our faithful subjects.'[8] The letter, of course, protests far too much; but it does reveal a general truth – that submission and service had to be earned and won, and that by effort, suavity and persuasion. Indeed the arrangements so made were often in the nature of treaties of friendship as much as submissions: an English contemporary chronicler catches their spirit when he describes Llywelyn ab Iorwerth, prince of Gwynedd (d. 1240), as 'the confidant and friend' (*familiaris et amicus*) of Earl Ranulf of Chester, while the *Annals of Connacht*, though they have got the historical facts wrong, capture the same sentiment when they refer to William Marshal as 'personal friend' of Áed Ó Conchobair (Aed O'Connor) of Connacht (d. 1228).[9]

Áed Ó Conchobair and Llywelyn ab Iorwerth both found the fleshpots of the courts of the Anglo-Normans enticing. They were by no means alone in this. The Anglo-Normans had style and wealth; their courts opened a window onto a world of chivalry and courtoisie which must have been attractive and intoxicating for many of the native Welsh, Irish and Scottish dynasties and magnates. Historians, so it seems to me, have been slow to recognize as much. Puritanical in their own tastes and severely academic in their explanations, they have rarely given sufficient credit to the social appeal of the Anglo-Norman courts – of sitting at high table, as it were – in the process of domination. The Anglo-Normans knew otherwise; they wined and dined the natives and intoxicated them with their *mores*, knowing full well that flattery and food can do wonders for men's attitudes. Henry II went straight for the palates and *amour-propre* of the Irish chiefs: he commissioned them to construct a wickerwork palace in Dublin at Christmas 1171, invited the native princes there, fed them unheard-of dishes (which they dared not refuse), and left them gawping in amazement at 'the sumptuous and plentiful fare of the English table and the most elegant service by the royal domestics'.[10] It was a gastronomic, and thereby cultural, *coup de théâtre*. It was frequently repeated

---

[8] T. D. Hardy (ed.), *Rotuli Litterarum Patentium ... Vol. 1. part 1 : 1201–16*, (London, 1835), p. 191.

[9] *Annales Monastici*, vol. III, p. 82; *Annals of Connacht*, (as cited above, ch. 2, n. 60) pp. 24–5. Cf. *ibid.*, p. 9: 'Each one of them (the Galls of Ireland) was a friend to him (Áed) on his father's account as well as his own, since he, like his father before him, was liberal of wages and gifts to them.'

[10] *Expugnatio*, pp. 96–7 (Bk 1, ch. 33); Howden, *Chronica*, vol. 2, p. 32.

in Wales and Ireland: the prince of Powys was entertained at dinner by Henry II and the prince of Deheubarth shared the bishop of Hereford's table with the chief justiciar; while in Ireland Cathal Crobderg Ó Conchobair (Cathal Crovderg O'Connor), king of Connacht 1189–1224, spent the Christmas festival in 1211 at the house of the royal justiciar in Dublin.[11] Such dinner parties were, indirectly, as much concerned with the etiquette of submission and social assimilation as they were with teaching good table manners. That is why the English in Thomond were so anxious to persuade Muirchertach Ó Briain (Murtough O'Brien), king of Thomond 1313–43, and his men to spend 'the convivial season of Christmas' with the chief butler, where they might 'be entertained by him with all civility'.[12] It was the same thinking that lay behind the invitation to leading Welshmen to send 'their children and others of their kindred to the king, to be of his company, for the king has long desired it'.[13] Such social guardianship had both a custodial and a civilizing aspect. Gerald of Wales observed shrewdly that attending court was one of the routes along which Norman ideas and habits were channelled to the Welsh.[14] He was certainly right; but he might also have noted that the sense of social obligation and cultural inferiority involved in such visits was not without significance in the strategy of subjection.

Those who were invited to dinner might even be groomed for higher things. Henry I once again showed how it should be done. Having enticed the head-strong Owain ap Cadwgan to come into his peace, the king further mollified him with this seductive promise: ' "come with me and I will reward thee as may be fitting. And this I will tell thee: I am going to Normandy, and if thou wilt come with me, I will fulfil to thee everything that I have promised thee. And I will make thee a knight" '.[15] The conversation may be imaginary, but the tactics most certainly were not. The career of David, the youngest brother of the king of Scotland, is there to prove it: Henry I pampered him, entertained him lavishly at his court, trained him as a knight, took him with him to Normandy, rewarded him with a small lordship in the Cotentin and with lands in Yorkshire, appointed him a royal justice, gave him an earldom, and endowed him with a very rich widow as wife. Orderic Vitalis' comment said it all: 'loaded with gifts, he (David) sat at the king's side among the great magnates'.[16] Henry I's extraordinary largess was surely not disinterested. He had cocooned David in a web of munificence and obligation which should

11 Butler (ed.), *Autobiography of Giraldus Cambrensis*, pp. 82–3; *Itin. Kambrie*, pp. 144–5 (Bk 2, ch. 12); Annals of Clonmacnoise quoted in W. L. Warren, 'King John and Ireland' in Lydon (ed.), *England and Ireland in Later Middle Ages*, pp. 30–1.

12 *Caithréim*, vol. II, p. 69.   13 *Anc. Corr. conc. Wales*, p. 254.

14 *Descr. Kambrie*, p. 218 (Bk 2, ch. 7).

15 *Brut*, p. 38.

16 K. J. Stringer, *Earl David of Huntingdon 1152–1219* (Edinburgh, 1985), p. 2; G. W. S. Barrow, *David I of Scotland (1124–1153). The Balance of New and Old*, The Stenton Lecture (Reading, 1985), pp. 16–17; Orderic Vitalis, *Historia Ecclesiastica*, vol. IV, pp. 274–5.

bring its reward amply if and when David succeeded to the throne (as he did in 1124). Of the catalogue of favours none was perhaps more significant than that of initiating the young David into the order of knighthood. It opened the door into an exhilarating international world of aristocratic fellowship and customs. The appeal of this glittering world and its busy social calendar must have been well nigh irresistible. And who better to provide a formal introduction to it than the Norman and Angevin kings of England? One of the first to be so initiated was Duncan, future king of Scotland, who was knighted by Robert Curthose in 1087. His brother, David, was apprenticed as a knight in Henry I's court. David's grandson and successor as king, Malcolm IV (1153–65), showed an almost indecent anxiety to be girded with the belt of knighthood: snubbed by Henry II at Carlisle in 1158, he followed the king all the way to Toulouse the next year and was duly rewarded by being dubbed a knight at Périgueux, in the very heartland of the world of international chivalry. What fascination that world exercised over the Scottish royal house was further shown when William the Lion crossed over to Normandy in 1166 and took part in the tournament season, while four years later in May 1170 William's brother and heir presumptive, David, was knighted by Henry II at Windsor. The future Alexander II (1214–49) was similarly knighted by King John in London in March 1212 and his son, Alexander III (1249–86), by Henry III at York on Christmas day 1251.[17] Such a catalogue of the conferment of knighthood is surely not without significance in understanding the psychology of dependence: it opened the door onto a much more sophisticated, international world; it was also an acknowledgement of the social and hierarchical (if not constitutional) inferiority of the Scottish dynasty *vis à vis* the rulers of England, in whose court and at whose good time the ceremony took place. But at least the kings of Scotland had been admitted into the charmed circle. Very few indeed of the native rulers of Wales and Ireland were so admitted.[18] That spoke volumes of the king of England's views of their social polish and political weight.

Knighthood was one route to social assimilation and subjection; marriage was obiously another. Its function in this respect was fully recognized by contemporaries. It could be used to defuse tension and build up amity; that is what Orderic Vitalis had in mind when he referred to 'the sweetness of a marriage alliance'.[19] When Rhys ap Maredudd, the last native prince of Deheubarth (d. 1292), was wed to Ada Hastings the aim of the match was

---

[17] Anderson, *Scottish Annals*, pp. 104, 156, 240 (but cf. Anderson, *Early Sources of Scottish History*, pp. 240–3), 244 n. 2, 246, 330, 364.

[18] Among possible Welsh examples were Owain ap Cadwgan of Powys in 1114 (*Brut*, p. 38), Dafydd ap Llywelyn of Gwynedd in 1241 (*Annales Monastici*, vol. I, p. 115) and Dafydd ap Gruffudd of Gwynedd (who, according to *Eulogium Historiarum*, Rolls Series (3 vols., London 1858–63), vol. III, p. 144, was knighted 'contra morem gentis sue'). King John knighted Donnchad Cairprech Ó Briain of Thomond in 1210, *NHI*, vol. II, p. 130.

[19] *Historia Ecclesiastica*, vol. IV, pp. 202–3.

specifically said to be to bring to an end 'the major enmities and mortal wars between the kinsmen and ancestors' of the two partners.[20] A marriage could also be used for more positive purposes, to smooth and legitimize the process of penetration or, in Gerald of Wales' words, to put down deeper roots in the locality.[21] Access to resources and aid was also often a prime motive: when Arnulf of Montgomery solicited the hand of the king of Munster's daughter in 1102 what he had his eye on was the 'many armed ships' which her father sent with her,[22] just as John de Courcy, the conqueror of Ulaid, took the daughter of the king of the Isle of Man to wife in order to have the use of the fleet of her father, and later that of her brother, for his enterprises. Such marriages characterized the Anglo-Norman penetration of the British Isles from earliest days. For example, Gerald of Windsor had taken the seductive Nest, daughter of the prince of Deheubarth, to wife, by about 1100, while Cadwgan ap Bleddyn (d. 1111) of Powys returned the compliment by choosing the daughter of Picot de Sai of Shropshire ('the Frenchwoman' as she was called)[23] as one of his partners. Likewise in Ireland the pattern is repeated: one of the early invaders, William de Burgh, took the daughter of Domnall Mór Ó Briain (Donal O'Brien) (d. 1194) of Munster as his wife, while the Mac Carthaig king of Desmond, Ó Briain's rival, married Petronella Bluet, the daughter of the sheriff of Waterford and Cork.[24] In Scotland again, native families, such as the earls of Fife, quickly formed marriage bonds with the Anglo-Norman settlers. Such marriages were common not merely among the top ranks of the Anglo-Norman invaders, but also among their immediate followers – leading vassals such as Turberville, Baskerville, Sully and so forth in Wales.

These mixed marriages were crucially important in helping Anglo-Normans and natives to adjust to each other, to borrow each other's social customs and to begin the process of cultural integration. The hybrid names that they gave to their children demonstrate the process at work; so likewise do the arrangements for the 'native' widows of Anglo-Norman *conquistadores* such as Strongbow or John de Courcy to enjoy a dower-share of their husband's property in England.[25] But those marriages have an interest beyond that of mutual cultural adaptation, of creating a 'community of outlook';[26] they also reveal an attempt to evolve a deliberate strategy of peace and co-existence in the relationships between natives and Anglo-Normans. Thus when we find the Lord Rhys of Deheubarth (d. 1197) marrying his eldest son to a Braose and his daughters into leading Norman families such as Carew,

20 *Litt. Wallie* (Cardiff, 1940), pp. 92, 101.   21 *Itin. Kambrie*, 91 (Bk 1, ch. 12).

22 *Brut.*, p. 23.   23 *Brut*, pp. 31, 45.

24 For Petronella Bluet's marriage Warren, 'King John and Ireland', p. 29; for the theme in general K. Nicholls, *Gaelic and Gaelicized Ireland in the Middle Ages* (Dublin, 1972), pp. 16–17.

25 Davies, *Conquest*, p. 102; K. Nicholls in *Peritia*, vol.1 (1982), 381–2; M.-T. Flanagan, 'Strongbow, Henry II and Anglo–Norman Intervention', 70–4.

26 Duncan *Scotland*, p. 126.

Camville or Martin, or when we find Llywelyn the Great of Gwynedd (d. 1240) concluding a marriage agreement for his daughter with the earl of Chester's nephew and heir and doing so in order to obtain 'a lasting concord' with the earl, we seem to have left the world of conquest and confrontation far behind us.[27] The social integration which could be represented by such marriages and by the policies and attitudes that lay behind them could have immense political consequences. It might have opened up in Wales and Ireland the road to peaceful penetration and accommodation so successfully paved in Scotland.

But marriage, like knighthood, could be a subtle instrument of domination as well as of social integration. It is difficult to believe that all the marriages between the Anglo-Normans and the native Welsh and Irish were freely concluded. Several, one may suspect, were hurriedly arranged to buy off a military threat or to give a veneer of legality to an usurpation. We may, perhaps, catch their character most clearly in the bargain which Áed Buidhe Ó Néill (d. 1283) of Tír Eóghain struck with the earl of Ulster in 1269. Ó Néill was confirmed in his kingship, handed over hostages and gave a tribute; almost as an afterthought he was given a kinswoman of the earl as a bride and warned to treat her properly.[28] Marriage was woven into a strategy of subjection, however honourable. The same was true at the most exalted level of relationships. William the Lion of Scotland had good cause to know that. Unlucky or foolish enough to have been captured by Henry II in 1174, William tasted the bitter fruit of humiliation – albeit masquerading as a marriage feast – in September 1186. His bride was chosen for him by Henry II and was a kinswoman of his; the marriage was celebrated in the royal chapel at Woodstock by the archbishop of Canterbury; and it was the king of England who met the cost of the four days of wedding festivities and paid part of the dowry. Delightful as the occasion was, 'the very many earls and barons of the kingdom of England ... and several earls and barons of the kingdom of Scotland' who, we are told, attended could have been under no illusion that it was an exercise in political masterfulness and subjection.[29] Edward I repeated the exercise in very similar form for Llywelyn ap Gruffudd, prince of Wales, almost a century later. Having comprehensively defeated Llywelyn in 1277 and imposed the most abject terms on him, Edward I now ostentatiously displayed the magnanimous face of domination and victory. He arranged for Llywelyn to be married to his bride, Eleanor de Montfort (whom Edward had previously captured and detained), in Worcester cathedral on St Edward's day, the

[27] E. Owen (ed.), *Catalogue of Manuscripts relating to Wales in the British Museum.* Cymmrodorion Record Series (4 vols., London 1900–22), vol. II, p. 357; vol. III, p. 526; R. C. Christie (ed.), *Annales Cestrienses*, Lancashire and Cheshire Record Society (1857), pp. 52–3.

[28] *Record of the MSS of Lord De L'Isle and Dudley*, Historical Manuscripts Commission, Vol. 1 (1925), pp. 31–2.

[29] Anderson, *Early Sources of Scottish History*, pp. 310–11; Anderson, *Scottish Annals*, pp. 288–9, 293–4.

feast-day of the English monarchy; the magnates of England were there by invitation and so were the king and queen of Scotland; Edward and his brother Edmund gave away the bride; and Edward also met the cost of the wedding feast and of conveying Eleanor's goods to the Welsh border. It was an act of political subjection dressed up as social munificence.[30]

The giving of gifts was likewise part of the same process. It is true that we may regard some of the furs, saddles, robes, falcons and hounds given as no more than the obligatory gifts of the social round. Such, for example, was the expense allowance and a robe of the king's gift granted to the Irish chief of the ÓhAnluain (O'Hanlon) clan when he travelled from Uriel to see the justiciar in Dublin, or the robes and cask of wine with which the earl of Norfolk almost literally lubricated relationships with the tempestuous Mac Murchada of the Wicklow mountains.[31] The native lords were no doubt duly flattered by such munificence and could hardly wait to show off their gifts. As Gerald put it, 'each of them returned to their own land with honour, taking with them the presents given them by the king'.[32] But more often than not the distribution of gifts was not an act of social charity but the due reward for acknowledging subjection. In the episode recounted by Gerald, the presents were only distributed *after* all the princelings of southern Ireland had made their voluntary submission. The king and his officers knew full well what they were about – giving robes, furs and saddles in return for submission or 'spending much money in drawing into the king's peace divers petty kings'.[33] It was domination by munificence or, as a Welsh chronicler put it sourly, 'deceiving with promises, as it was the custom of the French'.[34] But in truth the bribes and gifts of the Anglo-Normans were well-nigh irresistible to the impoverished and cashless members of native Welsh and Irish dynasties, especially those – and they were always considerable in number – who felt themselves deprived of due status and territorial wealth. Thus it is not difficult to realize how the fortunes of Owain Brogyntyn of Powys were transformed – and his political position compromised – by the £150 or so he received from Henry II's treasury in the years 1159–69. Owain Brogyntyn's uncle, Iorwerth Goch, compromised himself even further by accepting the most secure form of retainership, that of land in the form of a number of manors in Shropshire. He was not alone in being the beneficiary of such territorial munificence: the manor of Ellesmere (co. Salop) was used by the Angevins as a reward for members of the house of Gwynedd, while a number of leading Scottish aristocrats likewise came to enjoy English lands by gift.[35] But, of course, the premier example was the honour of Huntingdon, a vast complex of estates in east midland England,

30 J. B. Smith, *Llywelyn ap Gruffudd, Tywysog Cymru* (Caerdydd, 1986), p. 321.
31 *CDI*, vol. III, p. 70; R. Frame, 'The Justiciar and the Murder of the MacMurroughs in 1282', *Irish Historical Studies*, 18 (1972–3), 224–5.
32 *Expugnatio*, pp. 94–5 (Bk 1, ch. 32).   33 *CDI*, vol. I, pp. 273–4.   34 *Brut*, p. 39.
35 J. E. Lloyd, *History of Wales from Earliest Times to the Edwardian Conquest*, 3rd edn. (2 vols., London, 1939), vol. II, pp. 494, 520, 553, 616–17.

which was first granted to the young David of Scotland, along with his wife, in 1114, and which was held thereafter, whether in direct lordship or feudal superiority, by Scottish kings or by a cadet branch of the family until well into the thirteenth century. As Dr Stringer has remarked such grants were 'a well-tried technique of management in the political cupboard of the English crown'.[36]

We must, of course, beware of construing such relationships too cynically, of detecting the Trojan horse of Anglo-Norman domination behind every act of friendship and munificence. Our historical imaginations should be able to encompass genuine cordiality in relationships and mutual accommodation as well as confrontation and conquest. Gerald of Wales was able to compliment two Welsh princes, one in north Wales and the other in the south-east, for 'observing a strict neutrality between the Welsh and the English', and they were by no means exceptional.[37] Welsh chiefs could learn to address their writs – themselves in a form borrowed from England – 'to all their men French, English and Welsh'; they soon learnt to build mottes in the Norman fashion and even to erect stone castles; they were occasionally allowed to appear as witnesses to the benefactions of the Anglo-Norman lords; they even occasionally came to hold their lands by a modified form of feudal tenure known as Welsh knights' fees.[38] Many native families, with more of less conviction and with greater or lesser speed, trimmed their sails to the realities of the new world of Anglo-Norman power. Some, such as the Welsh dynasty of Powys, eased themselves into it by a series of marriages into Anglo-Norman families; others surrendered their native identity altogether, none more so than the Mac Gilla Mo Cholmóc of south Dublin who adopted the suitably Normanized name of Fitz Dermot.[39] Anglo-Norman lords for their part were also perfectly capable, if only for their own self-interest, of cultivating the arts of peace, friendship and conciliation. Maurice de Prendergast was known within a few years of his arrival in Ireland as 'Maurice of Ossory', because he had struck up such a cordial and mutually advantageous relationship with Mac Gilla Pátraic of Osraige; while Gilbert of Nangle fitted so well into his Irish surroundings that he was quickly known as Mac Costello and was richly rewarded by the ruler of Connacht.[40] Some of the demonstrations of mutual friendship were indeed remarkable: an Ó Conchobair and a de Burgh might share the same bed as a sign of peace, while in other cases newcomer and native publicly displayed amity by mixing their blood together in a common

[36] Stringer, *Earl David*, p. 19; also pp. 193–4 and n. 64.
[37] *Itin. Kambrie*, p. 145 (Bk 2, ch. 12).
[38] *Calendar of Charter Rolls* (6 vols., London, 1903–27), vol. II, p. 359; Dugdale, *Monasticon Anglicanum*, vol. IV, p. 596; 'Cartulary of Brecon Priory', *Archaeologia Cambrensis*, 4th series, vol. XIV (1883), pp. 146–7, 151; Davies, *Lordship and Society*, p. 76.
[39] Davies, *Conquest*, pp. 233, 235; *NHI*, vol. II, pp. 82–3, 445.
[40] *Song*, ll.1146–51; Orpen, *Ireland under the Normans*, vol. II, pp. 154–5.

vessel.[41] Nor should we be too cynical in interpreting such acts. There is no reason, for example, to doubt that Hugh de Lacy did indeed 'win the support of the Irish by generous treatment and flattering them with his friendship'[42] or that Llywelyn ab Iorwerth of Gwynedd and Earl Ranulf of Chester were genuine in their protestations of mutual respect and affection.

Anglo-Norman penetration, therefore, often insinuated itself along the channels of friendship, accommodation and affability; and native leaders often did much to ease its passage. Yet the Anglo-Normans ultimately had no intention, at least in Wales or Ireland, of being regarded merely as partners or as equals. What they were looking for was mastery; what they required therefore was submission and dependence. We need not, and should not, build great contractual or constitutional edifices on those two words. What was demanded was a clear and visual acknowledgement of dependence, underwritten, if possible and appropriate, by guarantees – notably the surrender of hostages and the exchange of gifts. The surrender of Malcolm III of Scotland (1058–93) to William the Conqueror at Abernethy in 1072 may serve as an example: 'he (Malcolm) came and made peace with King William and gave hostages and became his man'. That form of submission was repeated countless times, whether between the English king and native princes – as, for example, in the submission of King Malcolm IV of Scotland and a bevy of Welsh princelings to Henry II at Woodstock in July 1163 – or between Anglo-Norman lords and local chieftains – as, for example, in the submission of the Ó Néills to the Lacy or de Burgh earls of Ulster, in return for the retention of their kingship (*regalitas*).[43] We must be careful not to construe such relationships too legalistically or too much in the light of the hindsight informed by thirteenth-century feudal definitions. Submission most certainly was made; due respect or reverence shown; and superiority acknowledged. But the relationship was mutual and not necessarily regarded as grovelling. The overlord granted the dependant his peace, in other words treated him as a friend not as an enemy; he frequently confirmed him in the position he held (with neither party having too clear a view of what that meant, or being too anxious to define it); and he allowed him in Gerald's words to return 'to his own locality'. Such an act was not necessarily seen as demeaning or unwelcome: many a prince must have gone home, as Fedlimid Ó Conchobair is reported to have done from the king's court in 1240, 'joyfully and contentedly'.[44] No act of national or dynastic capitulation was necessarily involved. Indeed, on the contrary, an amicable and mutually profitable relationship had been initiated, its mutuality being sometimes very clearly spelt out (as in the indenture concluded between Ralph Pipard and

---

41 *Annals of Connacht*, pp. 139, 167.   42 *Expugnatio*, pp. 190–1 (Bk 2, ch. 21).
43 Anderson, *Scottish Annals*, p. 95; Katharine Simms in *Seanchas Ard Mhacha* 9 (1978–9), 77; H.M.C. *De L'Isle and Dudley*, pp. 31–2.
44 *Annals of Connacht*, p. 73.

Aonghus MacMathgamna (Mac Mahon) in the later thirteenth century in Uriel).[45]

Submission could be minimal, proceeding no further than an acknowledgement of superiority. Thus when Henry I was insinuating his way into the tumultuous politics of Powys in the early twelfth century, he tried to entice the princelings by offering a superiority 'without tribute and without castles' and 'without rent or payment'.[46] Yet the exceptional nature of the offer that Henry made on this occasion suggests clearly that more was normally involved in submission than metaphorical doffing of one's cap to the superior lord. Hostages, often the children of the ruling dynasty or leading noblemen of the region, were handed over into honourable custody. Such hostage-taking might be dressed up as invitations, but of the kind that could not be refused. Hostages were ultimately guarantors of continued political deference; many of them paid with their lives or their members to serve as a reminder of that dreadful point. Tributes, often very large tributes, were offered *prior* to submission as the price of being admitted into the peace of the king or overlord: Lord Rhys of Deheubarth bought his way into Henry II's favour in 1170 with a proffer to 4,000 oxen and 300 horses (though in an act of calculated magnanimity Henry only accepted the best 36 of them) while Áedh Ó Néill offered 3,500 cows to the earl of Ulster.[47] Nor were such tributes necessarily a once-and-for-all payment; tribute cattle were gathered on a more regular basis and served as a reminder of political subjection and its practical costs in the most valuable asset of a pastoral society.

Military service was another manifestation of the obligations entailed in subjection. After all what better way was there in a military society for a dependent ally to demonstrate his loyalty and to do so in the most public and useful manner? This was not military service in respect of land-tenure – land did not enter into the equation – but the military aid that any overlord could expect from a sworn dependant. So it was that Alexander I of Scotland accompanied Henry I on his Welsh expedition in 1114 or Malcolm IV Henry II on his campaign to Toulouse in 1159. The Lord Rhys curried favour with Henry II by dispatching his son to help the king in Normandy, while Llywelyn ab Iorwerth of Gwynedd tried to demonstrate his loyalty to John in 1209 by accompanying him to the Scottish border. The Irish princes quickly picked up the idiom of obedience: they tumbled over one another in their anxiety to prove their fidelity to John by accompanying him on his triumphal march through Ireland in 1210 and were no doubt duly flattered to be summoned (individually) to be ready for service in Scotland in 1244 or Gascony in 1254 and actually to serve in Wales in 1245. The Annals of Connacht catch the spirit of this military bond admirably when they report that, after his service in

[45] *Ormond Deeds*, vol. i, no. 268.   [46] *Brut*, pp. 38, 24. Cf. *Annals of Connacht*, p. 67.
[47] *Brut*, 66–7; H.M.C. *De L'Isle and Dudley*, p. 31.

Wales in 1245, 'Fedlimid (Ó Conchobair) was held in honour by the king then and was well pleased when he returned westwards'.[48]

Hostages, tributes and military service were, therefore, among the most common outward manifestations of dependence and of the acceptance of dependence. A much longer catalogue of obligations could, and would, be added to that list; but in the early generations of Anglo-Norman penetration of the British Isles, the *conquistadores* were often well content with what one may call the art of light dominance. Two features may be said to stand out about the nature of that dominance. First, it was spasmodic and fairly unstructured, rather than regular, systematic and exacting. Second, it did not, for the most part, extend into the spheres of land and justice, the twin routes along which overlordship was to be devastatingly intensified in the thirteenth century. Initially the Anglo-Norman kings and lords were well content with the personal acknowledgement of their domination and with periodic demonstrations of subjection which boosted their egos, filled their larders and augmented their armies.

Such subjection was by no means alien or objectionable to the Welsh and the Irish; that is why they adjusted to it so relatively easily. The rituals and terminology of submission were old-established features in the structuring of personal and political power in pre-Norman Wales and Ireland; failure to recognize as much, allied to a mechanical interpretation of that bogey (if not bogus) term, feudalism, has not infrequently led historians astray in interpreting the impact of Anglo-Norman lordship on native society in both countries. Clientship, submission (*gwrogaeth*), protection (*nawdd*), obligatory gift-giving and gift-receiving (*cyfarws*) and formal bonds of friendship (*carennydd, cymdeithas*) are among the most fundamental concepts which enable us to make sense of early Welsh royal and aristocratic society. They are replicated in the fuller, if often much later, Irish evidence and supplemented by formal rituals of submission – notably entry into the house of the superior and the acceptance of a gift (*tuarastal*) from him – and by well-defined notions of protection (*comairce*). Such ceremonies and terminology are in some ways reminiscent of those of the feudal world, provided – and it is an important proviso – that our picture of feudal relationships is a very fluid one and has been emptied of some of the rigid and anachronistic legalism that came to be associated with it. Concepts of domination and clientship in Wales and Ireland were highly elastic, ranging from the honourable to the demeaning, from the voluntary to the extorted. Obligations were certainly involved in such relationships; but they had not been cast in legal concrete. The assumptions were those of hegemony and clientship rather than those of direct or territorial lordship.[49]

---

[48] *Annals of Connacht*, p. 85.
[49] For Wales two articles by T. M. Charles-Edwards are fundamental, 'The Date of the Four Branches of the Mabinogi', *Transactions of the Honourable Society of Cymmrodorion*,

Such notions of hegemony and clientship informed not only relationships within the native polities of Wales and Ireland but also the relationships of the rulers of those polities with their powerful neighbours in England. This had certainly been so in pre-Norman days as far as Wales was concerned. Thus in 1056 Gruffudd ap Llywelyn (d. 1063), even in his hour of triumph, 'swore oaths that he would be a loyal and faithful under-king to King Edward (the Confessor)', while his successors in 1063 were even more fulsome, understandably so in the circumstances, in the terms of their submission, giving 'hostages to the king . . . swearing oaths to be loyal to him in all things, ready to serve him everywhere on sea and land and to render such tribute . . . as had formerly been paid to any other king'.[50] Anglo-Scottish relationships were likewise interpreted within much of the same framework. Scottish kings were either required to acknowledge their dependence (as was Malcolm III) or readily agreed to do so (as did Duncan II, Edgar and Alexander I) because they owed their thrones to the intervention and support of the English king.[51] When Henry II entered Ireland in 1171 it was precisely the same kind of hegemony that he claimed, nor were the Irish kings loath to concede it to him. Very much the same concepts of hegemony and submission informed the relationship of the greater Anglo-Norman lords with the princelings and leading men of their lordships in Wales and Ireland. Many of the leaders of native Leinster society, for example, were quickly enrolled as Strongbow's clients, while Áed Ó Néill (d. 1230) entered into a like dependence on John de Courcy and Hugh de Lacy, the Anglo-Norman lords of Ulster.[52]

We are prone to interpret submission as involving surrender and capitulation; contemporaries took a much more relaxed, positive and even optimistic view of it. It stabilized and formalized relationships, at least for a time. It confirmed the status of native rulers, albeit on a lower rung of the ladder of hierarchical authority. It in no way diminished the Lord Rhys' status within his own kingdom that he ruled it under the authority of Henry II (*sub rege principante*), nor was Ruaidrí Ó Conchobair's power in Connacht reduced by his acknowledgement that he was king 'under' Henry.[53] On the contrary, the support of a powerful patron could greatly enhance the standing of his client. It could do so at the level of the vicious segmentary conflicts within native dynasties. That was the prospect that Henry I's lieutenant held out to two of the ambitious princelings of Powys when he promised that 'he (the king) will honour and exalt you over and above your fellow land holders and he will

1970, pp. 263–98, esp. 274–9 and 'Honour and Status in some Irish and Welsh Prose Tales', *Ériu* 29 (1978), pp. 123–41. For Ireland K. Simms, *From Kings to Warlords* (cited above Ch. 1, n. 52), though dealing with a later period, is deeply illuminating.

[50] *Anglo-Saxon Chronicle*, pp. 186, 191.

[51] Duncan, 'The Earliest Scottish Charters', *Scottish Historical Review*, 37 (1958), 134–5; Barrow, *Kingship and Unity*, pp. 30–1.

[52] *Song*, ll.3210–7; K. Simms in *Seanchas Ard Mhacha* 9 (1978–9), 77.

[53] *Expugnatio*, p. 28 (Bk 1, ch. 21); Roger of Howden, *Chronica*, vol. II, p. 84.

make all your kinsmen envious of you'.[54] Likewise when Diarmait Mac Carthaig (Dermot MacCarthy) (d. 1185) of Desmond was in danger of being ousted from his kingdom by his eldest son, he was not slow to remind the Anglo-Normans 'that he was the liege man and loyal subject of the king of England'.[55] A powerful patron could also help to liberate a local leader from the control of a neighbouring dynasty or a provincial king. Nor should it be forgotten that a well-timed submission to the king of England was one of the best guarantees of stemming the greed of the Anglo-Norman *conquistadores*. Thus the Irish kings in 1170 sent a delegation to Henry II asking him for protection 'from the insolence and tyranny of Earl Richard' (Strongbow); while the Lord Rhys' timely submission to the same king in 1171–2 was a masterly act, since it was clearly followed by a royal prohibition on further raids on Rhys' kingdom and severe punishment for those (such as young Mortimer) who dared to defy such a prohibition.[56]

Viewed in this light, submission looks much more attractive than it is often presented by historians. Irish kings and rulers, for example, rarely denied the lordship of the king of England. It was not political subjection, but the unlawful expropriation of their lands, which they resented. Indeed what is striking is the almost pathetic fashion in which native rulers, such as those of Connacht and Thomond in the early thirteenth century, curried favour with the English crown, seeking its protection, promising faithful service, and making what appear to us outrageously bad bargains in order to secure formal grants of the remains of their attenuated kingdoms.[57] Their anxiety to please, to demonstrate their 'friendship' and to forward their petitions speak of a real anxiety to come to terms with the Anglo-Norman world and to mould it to the image of their own. What they wanted, what they thought or hoped they had got, was an *ard-ri*, a high king, who would protect them. Submitting to such a ruler was eminent good sense, indeed an honour.

Submission also generally served the needs of the superior lord well enough. Permanent military occupation was neither feasible not financially worthwhile, especially when there were richer pickings, and constant distractions, elsewhere. Notions of legal uniformity and a machinery for administrative control at a distance were likewise in their infancy. What an overlord, be he king or aristocrat, wanted was an acknowledgement of his mastery, underpinned by the payment of an occasional, or even an annual, tribute. Such a relationship may appear rather insubstantial and somewhat tenuous; and so indeed it was. It had to be frequently lubricated by parleys and social visits, repaired by renewed protestations of friendship and good behaviour, and reinforced by new submissions. The story of the relationship of Henry II with

---

54 *Brut*, p. 29.   55 *Expugnatio*, pp. 164–5 (Bk 2, ch. 14).
56 Gervase of Canterbury, *Historical Works*, ed. W. Stubbs, Rolls Series (2 vols., London, 1879–80), vol. I, p. 235; Davies, *Conquest*, pp. 275, 291.
57 See below p. 100–1.

Lord Rhys of Deheubarth after their *détente* in 1171–2 shows this all too clearly: the relationship was constantly under strain and had to be recurrently repaired by parleys, negotiations, visits to the king's courts, calculated acts of friendship, the surrender of hostages and the renewal of fealty. Yet in spite of everything it survived for eighteen years. It did so because it suited the interests of both parties.[58]

The same is true of scores of other agreements, most of them unrecorded, between Anglo-Norman lords and the leaders of native society in Wales and Ireland. What the newcomers wanted – especially in the upland districts of lordships such as Gwent, Glamorgan or Brycheiniog (Brecon) or in the inaccessible interiors of eastern Meath and Leinster – was to establish a working relationship with local society and to draw its leaders into a framework of deference and minimal obedience. The authority of such leaders was confirmed; indeed it would be enhanced by being formally underwritten by Anglo-Norman lords and kings. So it was, for example, that Lord Rhys, once he had submitted to Henry II, was appointed 'justice on his behalf in all Deheubarth'; just as the so-called Treaty of Windsor three years later confirmed Ruaidrí Ó Conchobair's right to discipline (*justitiet*) the inhabitants of the land under his authority.[59] It was, to borrow a famous phrase, self-government at the king of England's command. In truth there was no alternative. The lines of medieval government could not be indefinitely extended, and (as the vassals of the earl of Pembroke put it) 'it is not easy to control the Welsh except through one of their own race'.[60] Indeed one could take a more positive view of such a policy: what better way was there to suck the leaders of native society into the Anglo-Norman world – and to test their loyalty – than by entrusting them with responsibilities on behalf of the new rulers, even to the extent of appointing them guardians of the new Norman castles – as at Carmarthen in 1116 or in the equally strategic fortress of Carrigogunnell near Limerick in John's reign.[61]

Submission, therefore, opened up the prospect of establishing an effective working relationship between the Anglo-Normans on the one hand and their Welsh, Irish and even Scottish clients on the other. For the Anglo-Normans submission was well adapted to what they initially required and deemed practical; it was also a strategy which they had employed to good effect on the continent to build their 'empire'. It had the further advantage that it could be intensified and given a more demanding and threatening aspect as occasion required and opportunity suggested. For the Welsh and the Irish submission was a familiar concept within the intensely competitive world and temporary hegemonies of native politics. It allowed them to adjust to the fast-changing

---

[58] Davies, *Conquest*, pp. 222–3, 290–1.
[59] *Brut*, p. 68; Roger of Howden, *Chronica*, vol. II, p. 84.
[60] *Anc. Corr. conc. Wales*, p. 48.
[61] *Brut*, p. 41; Orpen, *Ireland under the Normans*, vol. II, p. 244.

fortunes of that world and to do so on terms which enabled them to acknowledge dependence without surrendering too much of the substance of their own authority. If submission proved such a supple instrument within the power struggles of native politics, there was every reason to believe that native leaders would use it to equal advantage to come to terms with the hegemonic claims of the Anglo-Normans. And this is indeed what we find. To that extent there is a far greater continuum from the world of native politics to that of Anglo-Norman domination than the chronologies and assumptions of our national historiographies often concede.

Indeed one may go further and wonder whether, within this framework of submission and non-interventionist hegemony, native societies could not have come to terms with the Anglo-Normans. In other words might we not be talking of accommodation rather than conquest, of a *modus vivendi* rather than an *expugnatio*? That, for example, is what we find in south-east Wales. The native Welsh dynasty there quickly came to terms with the Anglo-Normans, witnessed their deeds, even took charge of the castle of Usk, referred deferentially to the earl of Gloucester as 'our lord' and collected handsome sums from the royal exchequer for loyal service. But the dynasty kept its options open and went occasionally on the rampage through lowland Gwent to show that its power was by no means spent and that any promise of deference was contingent on the lord's good behaviour. What needs to be emphasized above all for our purposes is that here, on the very borders of Wales, a *modus vivendi* between Anglo-Norman lords (occasionally supported by the king) and the native Welsh dynasty survived for well over a hundred and fifty years and could easily have blossomed into a permanent pattern of co-existence and political assimilation.[62]

It is a pattern which is repeated time and again throughout Wales and Ireland as accords were reached, compromises struck and realities recognized, especially at the local level. The experience of Scotland is there to remind us that the Anglo-Normans could adjust sensitively and successfully to the existing dispensation and be gradually assimilated into it. There are indications a-plenty of how bridges might have been built between natives and incomers in Wales and Ireland likewise. Welsh chiefs occasionally appeared as witnesses of the deeds of Anglo-Norman lords; a few Welsh and Irish leaders came to hold land by feudal service and to appear at the courts of Norman lords; and, as we have seen already, marriage, military service and social invitations further promoted the opportunities for accommodation and integration. Above all what was required if the two communities were to be successfully integrated was that a sensitive respect be shown for the rights and status of native leaders. Those leaders craved good lordship; above all they craved the security, the attention and the patronage which they regarded as the

---

62 Crouch in *Morgannwg*, 29 (1985), pp. 20–41 (cited above ch. 2, n. 2). Cf. the behaviour of the Mac Murchada dynasty in Leinster.

due and proper return for their submission and loyalty. So it was that they travelled to Dublin to remind the justiciar and his colleagues there of their loyal service or plied the king and his officials with petitions and protests. The king was certainly by no means deaf to their representations. He could strike workable accords with them, as Henry II did very successfully with Lord Rhys of Deheubarth; he could also give them a clear title to their lands and promise that they would not be disseised without the judgement of the king's court, as King John promised Cathal Crobderg of Connacht in an infamous charter in September 1215.[63] He could show a due respect for their sensibilities and sense of self-importance by addressing some of his important public announcements to them. The king and his officials could also flatter them with rewards and titles. That is how the justiciar of Ireland pampered Domnall son of Art Mac Murchada (MacMurrough), self-styled king of Leinster, in the early fourteenth century – giving him robes and a fee 'for good service done and to be done in the future'; granting him the custody of a royal manor; persuading him to join an expeditionary force to Scotland; and, highest compliment of all, according him the status of banneret.[64] Anglo-Norman lords, likewise – and indeed even more so – could strike very workable accords with native leaders, entertain them in their courts and include them in their social rounds. Had such approaches been systematically built upon, it is not inconceivable that a political community might eventually have been forged which embraced the native leaders of Wales and Ireland, or at least a goodly number of them, within its ambit. Had that happened then the history of the British Isles might have taken a very different direction. Gaelic chiefs and Welsh princelings would have found a source of patronage and protection in the king of England's court; they would have had the feeling of being members of a family, sharing in its social round and participating in its political dialogue.

But it was not to be. 'Distinction and diversity' (to borrow the phrase of the so-called Act of Union of England and Wales of 1536), rather than accommodation and integration, were ultimately to be the dominant themes of the relationships of the English crown and aristocracy with the native societies of Wales and Ireland. The reasons why this was so are deeply embedded in the history of the thirteenth and fourteenth centuries. Some of them are to be found within the native polities of Wales and Ireland, especially as the illusions of their rulers were shattered and their pretensions and ambitions transformed. In neither country – and here the contrast with Scotland stands out starkly – did the nature of the Anglo-Norman penetration or the structures and habits of fragmented native political societies allow the development of a single political orbit within which both natives and incomers could move; in neither was there a single political centre or authority which could have served

---

[63] *CDI*, vol. I, pp. 100–1; see below, p. 100.
[64] R. Frame, 'English Officials and Irish Chiefs in the Fourteenth Century', *English Historical Review* 90 (1975), 768–9.

as a source of patronage and adjudication for both parties; in neither did a single custom, a common law, emerge by which both parties could be bound and protected. Other reasons for the ultimate failure of the road of accommodation are to be found in the character and tempo of the Anglo-Norman penetration of Wales and Ireland. That penetration, though it could be devastatingly rapid especially in its earlier stages, lacked the momentum and the stamina to overwhelm either country completely. The piecemeal, long-drawn-out and uncompleted character of both conquests was an unpropitious basis on which to build permanent accord. Military men still set the tone and called the tune. The prospect of workable settlements was recurrently shattered by raids and counter-raids, which in their turn added to the catalogue of mistrust and to the accumulated memories of treachery. The Anglo-Normans charged the Welsh and Irish with perfidy, instability and fecklessness; while the natives responded in kind, claiming, in the words of the Welsh chronicle, that 'none of the Welsh dared place trust in the French'.[65] The English crown might have stepped in and imposed a settlement which sought to balance the claims and ambitions of both parties. Indeed it did so periodically: Henry II imposed his will magisterially on native prince and Anglo-Norman lord in both Wales and Ireland; and King John showed, at least spasmodically, a similar imaginativeness and even-handedness in his policies in Ireland. Both kings were moved by an anxiety for some modicum of peace on the outer edges of their empires and by a well-founded mistrust of the ambitions of some of their greater barons. Yet ultimately the crown was not neutral in these matters: it itself had an important stake, territorially and militarily, in both Wales and Ireland, and in both countries it could act as no more than a temporary brake, if that, on the insatiable acquisitiveness of the Anglo-Norman baronage.[66] After all, the barons who were carving lordships for themselves in Wales and Ireland were also territorial magnates in England and among the leading confidants and advisers of the king.

But there remains one other reason why no *modus vivendi* could eventually be worked out. It rests in the very theme of this chapter, submission, and in the mutual misunderstanding of what it entailed. As so often, it is in the world of perceptions and expectations that the breakdown in relationships is best comprehended. Both parties – as in other societies which have had to try to come to terms with the prospect of domination and conquest – lived under illusions. The Anglo-Normans assumed that their agreements with Welsh and Irish rulers could be assimilated to relationships with which they were familiar elsewhere. The so-called Treaty of Windsor of 1175 is perhaps the most striking example of the monumental illusion involved in such a belief. It tried

---

[65] *Brut*, p. 71 (1175).

[66] The dilemma is equally clear in Richard II's policies in Ireland in the 1390s, E. Curtis, *Richard II in Ireland 1394–5* (Oxford, 1927); D. Johnston, 'Richard II and the submissions of Gaelic Ireland', *Irish Historical Studies*, 22 (1980), pp. 1–20.

to apply the concepts of feudal obligations, territorial power and judicial responsibility to the shifting and fluid world of Irish power politics; it was little wonder that it was itself sucked into oblivion within a few years. Both the advisers of Henry II and historians have accorded it a constitutional status which, in truth, it could never hope to enjoy. But the Welsh and the Irish equally had their own illusions. They submitted, more or less readily, to Anglo-Norman kings and barons. They did so partly to save their own skins, but also because they believed that all that they had acknowledged was a loose hegemony and one which should indeed secure them protection against their enemies, native and foreign. The prolonged attempt of the rulers of Connacht to establish a working relationship with the English crown and to win security of tenure and inheritance for themselves is perhaps the most pathetic example of the pursuit of this illusion.[67] But it is by no means the only one. The depth of the illusion became even more profound as feudal relationships were more carefully defined and as written documents wove a web of obligations which both attracted and entangled clients in it. When the illusion was shattered and reality revealed for what it was, the reaction was one of outrage. It was the moment of truth for both parties: submission was the first stage not to accommodation nor even to hegemony, but to conquest. But before we turn to the theme of conquest, we need to look at the rôle of the king of England in the process of domination and at the ways the powers of overlordship might be intensified short of a complete military conquest.

[67] *NHI*, vol. II, pp. 161–6.

4

The kings of England and the domination of the British Isles

In our analysis of the Anglo-Norman domination of the British Isles the king of England has hitherto barely figured. Such an oversight is deliberate. For a century or so after the Normans arrived in England, the king apparently played a secondary and often reluctant role in the advance of Anglo-Norman power and domination into Wales, Ireland and Scotland. Some of the evidence, it is true, would seem to suggest otherwise. Boasts, threats and fears seem to register clearly the conviction that the king of England's authority encompassed, or could encompass, the whole of the British Isles. 'Wales', said the Anglo-Saxon chronicler in his obit on William the Conqueror, 'was in his domain, in which country he built castles and so kept its people in subjection. Scotland also he reduced to subjection by his great strength ... If he had lived only two years more he would have conquered Ireland.'[1] William Rufus indeed seemed intent on realizing this latter ambition: Gerald of Wales relates his boast that he would use his fleet to form a bridge from Britain to Ireland in order to facilitate the conquest.[2] Nor were these merely the boasts of idle moments. They represented a view of the world that was coming to be shared elsewhere in the British Isles. The native Welsh chronicler was certainly in no doubt: for him Henry I was 'the man who had subdued under his authority all the island of Britain and its mighty ones'. 'None', he added despairingly, 'can contend against him save God himself.'[3] Rhetorical flourishes, maybe; but words seemed to be matched by action. After all, William I had penetrated with his army to Abernethy on the Firth of Tay in 1072 to show Malcolm III of Scotland who was master; in 1081 his army reached St Davids in farthest west Wales; and there is no reason to doubt the contemporary story that Irish princes quaked in their shoes when they heard that the displeasure of the king of England was directed at them.[4]

The king of England, therefore, clearly had the means and possibly the ambition to make his power felt in the farthest parts of the British Isles. Anyone who forgot that truism could be rudely and forcefully reminded of it: thus Rufus' expedition to Lothian in 1091 quickly brought Malcolm III once

---

[1] *Anglo-Saxon Chronicle*, p. 220 (*s.a.* 1086).   [2] *Itin. Kambrie*, pp. 109–10 (Bk 2, ch. 1).
[3] *Brut*, p. 42.   [4] William of Malmesbury as quoted above, p. 7.

more to his knees and his senses, while Henry I's two campaigns into Wales in 1114 and 1121 quickly reminded the resurgent Welsh princes of their relative impotence and vulnerability. Yet in spite of such occasional demonstrations of power and in spite also of contemporary hysterical fears that the king of England was plotting nothing less than the 'extermination of all the Britons',[5] the fact remains that the interest of the English kings in Wales, Ireland, and Scotland, was for the most part marginal and spasmodic. There is certainly little reason to believe that before the thirteenth century they contemplated what may be called a full-blown conquest of any of the three countries.

The reasons are not far to seek. Within the ambit of the territorial politics and ambitions of the Norman and Angevin kings, the outer margins of the British Isles were of secondary interest and concern compared with, say, the Vexin, Maine, Flanders, Boulogne or, later, Toulouse. Of the so-called 'Celtic' countries, Brittany was for obvious reasons much higher on the agenda of their political priorities than was Wales or even Scotland. This was reflected in the way that the dukes of Normandy had brought Brittany into the orbit of their power and again in the way that Henry II from 1156 onwards intensified his authority there, even to the extent of dividing the duchy into eight administrative districts and introducing Angevin legal practices.[6] Wales neither deserved nor received such close attention. There the Norman kings and their early Angevin successors were generally content with the acknowledgement of their ultimate overlordship, sometimes accompanied by the surrender of hostages and the payment of tribute.[7] Such overlordship was rarely specific in content; more often than not it was given at the end of a campaign, or the threat of one, rather than freely conceded at the beginning of a reign. Likewise, though the effective client status of the Scottish kings *vis à vis* the English monarchy from the time of William I onwards, especially in the years 1097–1124, could hardly be denied, the king of England showed singularly little anxiety to press the issue of his overlordship or to define it closely, except under the maximum provocation (as in 1174).[8] As for Ireland, in spite of the boasts of William Rufus and the menaces of Henry I, what is surely striking is the extreme reluctance of the English kings to be enticed thither. The bull *Laudabiliter* (1155), it is true, gave Henry II ample theoretical justification for intervention and he may have contemplated leading an expedition to Ireland in that year. But the initiative for the grant of *Laudabiliter* probably came from the church of Canterbury (which rightly feared for its claims to metropolitan control of

[5] *Brut*, pp. 37 (1114), 63 (1165).

[6] B.-A. Pocquet du Haut-Jussé, 'Les Plantagenets et la Bretagne', *Annales de Bretagne*, 53 (1946), pp. 1–27; J. Le Patourel, 'Henri II Plantagenet et la Bretagne', republished in J. Le Patourel, *Feudal Empires, Norman and Plantagenet* (London, 1984), ch. 10.

[7] The payment of an annual tribute of £40 by Rhys ap Tewdwr of Deheubarth recorded in *Domesday Book* vol. 1, p. 179a is an early example.

[8] Duncan, *Scotland*, pp. 254–5.

the Irish church), not from the king.[9] Henry II did not in fact go to Ireland for another sixteen years, and his expedition of 1171–2 was as much (if not more) concerned with demonstrating his authority over his ambitious Anglo-Norman barons there as with asserting his own overlordship of Ireland. He was certainly not contemplating a conquest of Ireland in the normally accepted sense of that word; and it was to be almost forty years before a king of England led another expedition to Ireland.

This impression of the very occasional and marginal interest that English kings showed in the outlying areas of the British Isles is confirmed by the absence of strong royal territorial interests there. The king was rarely without a territorial foothold in Wales and could occasionally (as in the reign of Henry I) extend his power there dramatically; but by 1200 direct royal interest was still confined to two enclaves around Carmarthen and Cardigan (only recently acquired) and even both of these were temporarily lost 1215–23.[10] In Ireland Henry II's bargain with Strongbow in 1171 had given him control of the key cities of Dublin, Waterford and Wexford and the surrounding districts; but even more than half a century later 'royal authority in Ireland could be rivalled by that of one or more territorial magnates'.[11] In Wales, Scotland and Ireland alike it was the Anglo-Norman barons – or rather a proportion of them – who set the pace and made the great territorial gains; not the king. He doubtless kept an eye on them, encouraged them (as Rufus appears to have done in Wales in 1093), was kept well informed of their activities, and sometimes stepped in to support them (with a quick military foray) or occasionally to restrain them. But in general terms he kept a fairly low profile; his major preoccupations were elsewhere.

Yet the kings of England did feel impelled on occasion to intervene in Wales, Scotland and, later, Ireland in the century or so after 1066. Their reasons for doing so were varied. The demands of security and a response to provocation were among them. If the Welsh or the Scots threatened England, led raids over the border (as the kings of Scots did, for example, in 1070, 1079, 1091, 1093, 1138 and 1174) or allied with disaffected elements in England (as the Welsh did 1067–9), then the security of the kingdom of England was threatened and an expedition might be mounted to counter the threat. Likewise if the momentum of Anglo-Norman aristocratic penetration seemed to be faltering, a royal expedition might serve to regenerate morale and recover the initiative. Such was probably the intention of William Rufus' two abortive campaigns into

[9] See in general M. Richter, 'The First Century of Anglo-Irish Relations', *History*, 59 (1974), pp. 195–210.

[10] R. R. Davies, 'Henry I and Wales', in *Studies in Medieval History presented to R. H. C. Davis*, ed. H. Mayr-Harting and R. I. Moore (London, 1985), pp. 132–47; Davies, *Conquest*, p. 289.

[11] R. Frame, 'Ireland and the Barons' War', in *Thirteenth-Century England, I. Proceedings of the Newcastle upon Tyne Conference 1985*, ed. P. R. Coss and S. D. Lloyd (Woodbridge, 1986), 160.

Wales in 1095 and 1097 or that of Henry I thither in 1114. When native princes got too big for their boots, a short and sharp royal expedition could quickly cut them down to size and remind them of the penalties for insubordination, as Henry I showed in Powys in 1121 and Henry II in Gwynedd and Deheubarth successively in 1157-8.

But royal attention was as likely to be drawn to Wales and Ireland by the over-ambitiousness of Anglo-Norman barons as by the obstreperousness of native princes. These barons were the king's subjects wherever they operated and he was ever watchful of their activities and pretensions. Indeed he was more watchful, to the point of paranoia, of their activities in Wales and Ireland precisely because it was in such frontier areas that their boundless ambition was most likely to blossom out of control and also out of sight. Thus it was to thwart the ambitions of the powerful Montgomery family (which had allied itself with the Welsh dynasty of Powys) that Henry I came to the Welsh borderlands in 1102 and it was through his own alliance with the Welsh that he completed his work so expeditiously. Likewise the prime motive for Henry II's expedition to Ireland in 1171-2 was to call Strongbow to book and to impose royal control on the process of conquest, on the conquerors as much as on the native Irish. Political mastery as much as empire building was at the root of the expedition. Exactly the same motives underlay the next royal expedition to Ireland, that of King John in 1210. In other words it was the complexities and suspicions of Norman and Angevin politics which often forced Wales and Ireland on the attention of the kings of England.

For at least the first century after the Norman conquest of England, royal policy towards Scotland, Wales and Ireland may, therefore, be broadly characterized as reactive, responding (often rather reluctantly and belatedly) to threats and invitations but rarely initiating action, least of all action which might be construed as a policy of royal conquest.[12] What the English king needed, it has been observed, was 'peace (by fear or friendship) with the Scottish king; [he] did not need conquest of the provinces of Scotland'.[13] In Wales, and later in Ireland, he was generally well content on the one hand with relatively stable relationships and on the other, where possible, with an acceptance of his overlordship. He was not even anxious for much of the time to press for a closer definition of that overlordship.

Such a formulation of the attitude of the Norman and Angevin kings towards Wales, Scotland and Ireland within the agenda of their concerns and priorities rings broadly true, at least for the twelfth century. Yet it is less than the whole truth, for the royal impact on the process of character of Anglo-Norman domination could take forms other than expeditions and direct intervention and territorial footholds. The Anglo-Norman penetration

[12] Cf. D. J. A. Matthew, *The Norman Conquest* (London, 1966), p. 222: 'It is unlikely that the Normans gave the conquest of Britain serious thought as a policy.'

[13] Duncan, *Scotland*, p. 255.

of Wales and Ireland may have been aristocratic enterprises, but they took place in a world whose nodal political and social focus was the king's court. The monarchy could – and did – make its power felt in a variety of practical and highly effective ways.

William the Conqueror taught that lesson to his barons in Wales at a very early date. He may indeed have given them a relatively free hand to acquire as much land as they could at the expense of the Welsh and doubtless exulted in their success; but equally he was not short of reminding them that his power extended fully into Wales. He made grants there 'in fee' and 'at farm', as Domesday Book shows; he took control of lands which had been appropriated without his formal permission; he stamped on rebellious barons and their vassals in Wales as he did elsewhere in his dominions and seized their forfeited estates into his hands; and he specifically reserved the lands of vacant Welsh bishoprics, and in effect the appointment of bishops, to himself. It was by his specific command that key castles such as Rhuddlan were built; and it was his coinage alone which was struck at the newly founded Norman mints in Wales. His march through south Wales to St Davids in 1081 demonstrated to Welsh prince and Norman baron that his authority in Wales brooked no limits or opposition.[14]

Henry II's expedition to Ireland in 1171–2 repeated the same lesson for native princes and settler barons in that country a century later. One of his preliminary acts *en route* to Ireland – the appointment of royal guardians to take charge of baronial castles in south Wales – showed his mood. Strongbow quickly rushed to make his submission and acknowledged that any lands he had conquered in Ireland were to be 'held of the king and his heirs'.[15] Henry regranted these lands to him, stipulating in a charter (which has not survived) that the service of one hundred knights was due from Leinster to the king, just as later he was to grant Meath to Hugh de Lacy for the service of fifty knights. Thus the Anglo-Norman conquerors of Ireland were firmly tied into a feudal nexus controlled by the king, indeed more securely bound than were the Marcher lords of Wales, since the titles of the Anglo-Norman lords in Ireland were based on written documents (not on ancient conquest) and included a specific quota of military service (whereas Norman lordships in Wales were held by unspecified services).

It was not only the occasional expedition which brought home the king of England's ultimate power over and in Wales and Ireland. The English barons in both countries were his vassals and he did not allow them to forget it. The feudal bond that tied them to the king afforded him recurrent opportunities to display his power over them and over their estates. If a baron died while his heir was still a minor, the wardship of the heir and the custody of his estates

[14] *Domesday Book*, vol. I, pp. 162, 269a; Orderic Vitalis, *Historia Ecclesiastica*, vol. IV, p. 139; G. C. Boon, *Welsh Hoards 1979–81* (Cardiff, 1986), pp. 40, 46.
[15] *Expugnatio*, pp. 90–1, 88–9 (Bk 1, ch. 29, ch. 28).

were at the king's disposal. So it was, for example, that the great lordships of Glamorgan and Gwynllŵg in south-east Wales were in the king of England's hands for at least sixty years in the period 1107–1243. Such custodies could greatly enhance the king's territorial power in both Wales and Ireland. Thus many of the great lordships of south Wales fell conveniently into Henry II's lap, at least temporarily, in the 1170s and 1180s; while King John's position in Ireland and his opportunity to influence the future of the English colony there were dramatically transformed in 1205–7, when premature baronial deaths gave him direct control of the whole of Tipperary and much of Limerick.[16] Custodies were a chilling reminder to baronial empire-builders of their vulnerability to ultimate royal control. They also provided the king with an opportunity to establish some of his own followers and retainers in the lordships in question and to introduce major administrative and legal reforms in them, often consciously based on royal models (as seems to have happened in Glamorgan, Pembroke and Munster).

Custodies depended on the accidents of baronial deaths and succession; on other occasions royal power manifested its might much more arbitrarily and devastatingly. The king's anger (*ira et malevolentia*) could destroy individuals and families as comprehensively in Wales and Ireland as in England or Normandy. Roger of Breteuil, the son of the powerful William fitz Osbern, earl of Hereford, found that out to his cost in 1075: among the estates that were confiscated in that year were the extensive lands that he and his followers had acquired in Gwent. The forfeiture of the estates of the great Montgomery family in 1102 was even more far-reaching in its impact on baronial power in Wales: the advance of the earl of Shrewsbury into central Wales was rudely terminated (thereby dramatically altering the pattern of Anglo-Norman penetration into Wales), while the crucial foothold that his brother, Arnulf of Montgomery, had established in farthest Pembroke was converted into a royal county. In Ireland it was John's reign which showed vividly how royal displeasure could transform the landscape of power at a stroke: among his major victims were John de Courcy (Ulster), William Braose (Limerick, as well as massive estates in Wales), and Walter and Hugh de Lacy (Meath and Ulster), while even the great William Marshal himself (lord of Leinster and earl of Pembroke) came within an ace of destruction. Even when the royal will was not so viciously malevolent as it was in John's reign, it could still exert a profound influence on the descent of landed estates in Wales and Ireland as elsewhere – denying the succession of a daughter here, securing the reversion of a key estate there and keeping an ever watchful eye on the territorial arrangements and ambitions of its baronage.

Kings could destroy individual barons and indeed whole families at a stroke; equally, they could raise men from the dust, especially for services rendered.

16 Davies, *Conquest*, p. 289; C. A. Empey, 'Settlement of the Kingdom of Limerick' (as cited above, ch. 2, n. 20), pp. 15–16.

Royal largess was the single most important factor in shaping and reshaping the fortunes of the Anglo-Norman aristocracy in Wales and Ireland in each successive generation in the twelfth and thirteenth centuries. In Wales, for example, Henry I, that consummate maker of men, planted many of his devoted followers in some of the key lordships of the March, promoting several of them by careful exploitation of one of the Crown's most invaluable sources of patronage – the control of the marriages of the daughters and widows of the king's feudal vassals.[17] In Ireland, Gerald of Wales' bragging about the achievements of his kinsmen may have concentrated historians' attention on aristocratic enterprise and initiative; but in truth it was royal munificence and favour which first opened the door of opportunity to many of the leading English families of medieval Ireland. It was the king (or John as lord of Ireland) who laid the foundations of the power of the future earls of Ormond in Munster through a handsome grant of five and a half cantreds to their lineal ancestor, Theobald Walter, in 1185; it was royal favour likewise which introduced men such as William de Burgh and Hamo de Valognes into Munster in the late twelfth century and bestowed vast lordships in Uriel on Gilbert Pipard and Bertram de Verdon at much the same time.[18]

Royal patronage may, it is true, have been a particularly formative influence in the early generations of the Anglo-Norman settlement of Wales and Ireland; but even in subsequent generations it had the opportunity and the means to effect a major re-ordering of the jigsaw of territorial power and to introduce new blood into both countries. For example, it was royal favour, and the needs of the political moment in England, which bestowed the great earldom of Ulster (under royal control since 1242) on Walter de Burgh in July 1263 or gave Thomas de Clare, younger brother of the earl of Gloucester and companion of Edward I, a major territorial stake in Ireland in 1276 through the grant of Thomond to him.[19] In an even more striking act of largess, Edward I used the occasion of his conquest of Wales to create four large new lordships in north-east Wales and to bestow them on some of his leading associates and confidants.[20]

In short the king of England had the power to make and unmake men in Wales and Ireland as elsewhere in his realms; he exercised that power recurrently and often high-handedly through the twelfth and thirteenth centuries. Nor was his intervention in these countries necessarily confined to the occasional military expedition, the initial grant of a lordship or of a right to conquer lands, the exploitation of feudal incidents, and periodic confiscations; it could also intrude itself more regularly into the affairs of Wales and Ireland

---

[17] Davies, 'Henry I and Wales', p. 142–7.

[18] Otway-Ruthven, *Ireland*, pp. 67–74 and the accompanying maps.

[19] Frame, 'Ireland and the Barons' War', pp. 164–5 (for revised dating and political context); M. Altschul, *A Baronial Family in Medieval England. The Clares 1217–1314* (Baltimore, 1965), pp. 187–95.

[20] Davies, *Conquest*, p. 363.

and into the activities of his barons there. The ordinary administrative, judicial and financial machinery whereby the king controlled the kingdom of England did not, it is true, extend into Wales. That persuaded English barons in Wales in later generations to make much of 'the liberties of the March' and to exploit their legal and fiscal immunities to keep the king's officers at arm's length. But the power of the king, or at least of a powerful king, was not to be inhibited by such administrative and legal niceties.

Both Henry I and Henry II showed as much clearly enough, not by grand constitutional declarations but by taking it for granted that their powers of intervention extended into Wales and, later, Ireland. Henry I confirmed the gifts of his barons in Wales; directed letters to his subjects there; confiscated, granted and withheld lordships there at his pleasure; and made royal estates, such as Carmarthen and Pembroke, answerable at his English exchequer.[21] Henry II went even further. He summoned the major lords of the March of Wales to an assembly and reminded them that their ambitions were ultimately subordinate to royal policy.[22] He followed threats by action – requiring the earl of Pembroke to restore a disinherited Welsh princeling, reprimanding the powerful William Braose for overstepping the mark in pursuit of his ambitions, and confiscating the estates of Roger Mortimer when his men dared to kill a Welsh chief travelling under a royal safe-conduct.[23] Royal power in Wales may have manifested itself much more spasmodically than in England in the twelfth and thirteenth centuries; it clearly lacked the institutional infrastructure that made the king's authority so routine and penetrative in Norman and Angevin England. Nevertheless it was real power for all that, and bared its teeth sufficiently frequently and menacingly to remind the Marcher barons of Wales that (as it has been said of Durham) 'royal sufferance was the basis' of such autonomy as they enjoyed.[24]

The king was prepared to suffer more in Wales than in Ireland. From the moment of his arrival in Ireland in 1171 Henry II made it abundantly clear that the new English lords there were not to be allowed as free a rein as their colleagues in Wales had come to enjoy. Lordships were to be held for specified feudal services. Indeed the rather open-ended charters which Henry II granted were quickly revised – as in the case of Munster and Leinster in 1208 – to make it clear that henceforth the king reserved to himself the pleas of the crown, jurisdiction in error and church lands even within the greatest liberties.[25] Grants were made which studiously reserved to the king 'all those things which belong to our royal crown'; while the contingent and provisional nature of royal gifts was underlined by a reminder to the grantee that the land 'should

21 Davies, 'Henry I and Wales', pp. 134–5, 145–6.
22 Stubbs (ed.), *Gesta Regis Henrici Secundi*, vol. I, p. 93.
23 Davies, *Conquest*, p. 275.
24 C. M. Fraser, 'Prerogative and the Bishops of Durham, 1267–1376', *English Historical Review*, 74 (1959), 474.
25 *CDI*, vol. I, p. 57; Otway-Ruthven, *Ireland*, pp. 182–3.

be surrendered to the king if he so required it'.[26] Only English law, the law of the king's court, was to prevail in English Ireland; there was to be no room there for the amalgam of local customs which had developed in Wales and whose existence as the law of March was formally acknowledged in Magna Carta in 1215. English Ireland was to be kept on a tighter rein in other ways: royal taxation in Ireland was levied from the late thirteenth century within and without liberties (whereas only once, in 1291–3, was a tax raised for the king from the Marcher lordships of Wales) and Irish liberties were expected to send representatives to the Irish parliament (whereas there was no parliamentary representation from the March of Wales until the sixteenth century).

The degree of institutional presence that royal power enjoyed in Ireland was therefore greater than in Wales; but that in no way gainsays the fact that both countries were part of the royal dominions. There was, of course, in general no conflict of interest between aristocratic enterprise and ultimate royal authority in Wales and Ireland, any more than there was in England. On the contrary, kings licensed and encouraged aristocratic entrepreneurship – as in the permission given to William Braose by King John to conquer as much land as he could from the Welsh, or in the licence granted to the earl of Gloucester 'to conquer all the lands he can from the Welsh, the king's enemies, without any claim by the king'.[27] Yet royal policy and aristocratic ambition did on occasion collide. Indeed they were possibly more likely to do so in areas such as Wales and Ireland, which lay outside the normal circuit of the king's itinerary and beyond the routine reach of his government. Even the lapse of a few years in Ireland could convert a royal protégé into a target of royal suspicion – as happened quickly to Hugh de Lacy, John de Courcy and others. Furthermore, a recurrent problem was posed by the need of the king to strike a balance between Anglo-Norman aristocratic acquisitiveness on the one hand and the yearning of native rulers for royal protection on the other.

Royal policy and attitudes in this respect fluctuated. When a king opted for détente with native princelings – as Henry II seems to have decided in Wales from the early 1170s – conflict with thrusting barons was well-nigh inevitable, even to the extent of using native leaders to thwart the plans of, and expel, the Anglo-Normans (as happened to William de Burgh in the pursuit of his claim to Connacht).[28] But, equally, if a king decided that it was in his interest to pursue war against the Welsh and the Irish, the localized interests of Anglo-Norman barons might not necessarily coincide with his ambitions. In that case, a king would ultimately have to insist on the overriding superiority of his wishes and policies to those of his barons. This was the lesson that Henry II seems to have taught two of the greatest Welsh Marcher lords, the

[26] *Rotuli Chartarum* (as cited above, ch. 2, n. 43), vol. 1, part 1, p. 84: Empey, 'Settlement of the Kingdom of Limerick', p. 5; *Close Rolls 1231–4*, pp. 524–5.
[27] *Rotuli Chartarum*, vol. 1, part 1, p. 66; *Calendar of Patent Rolls 1258–66*, p. 674.
[28] W. L. Warren, 'King John and Ireland' (as cited above, ch. 3, n. 11), 30.

earl of Gloucester and William Braose, and 'other of his barons of that country' (i.e. Wales), at a council in 1175 when he insisted that they were required to support any royal action in Wales in the event of a Welsh attack on the king's lands.[29] Again in 1245 Henry III's council insisted that Marcher lords were obliged to wage war against the Welsh when the king was on campaign.[30] Even in the remarkably autonomous and fragmented aristocratic world of the Welsh March it was the king of England who had the last – as indeed he had often had the first – word.

All in all royal power counted more, much more, in the process of the domination of Wales and Ireland than is sometimes suggested. That power, however, was variable in its attention and its intensity; it could appear detached, almost uninterested, in one decade, surprisingly interventionist in the next. One period in which the king of England pressed his claim to the lordship of the British Isles vigorously was in the reign of Henry II, notably during the first twenty years of his reign. It may be doubted whether it was a conscious policy. In good measure it was no more than part of Henry II's campaign to restore the *status quo* as it prevailed in 1135 and to recover all alienated or usurped royal rights; in part it arose from an anxiety for a closer definition and public recognition of overlordship. Henry meant to be master in the whole of his house, and when opportunity arose and the occasion demanded he was willing to display that mastery in no uncertain terms.

The king of Scotland was among the first to be taught that lesson. The kings of England regarded the kings of Scotland, to put it in the most flattering terms, as their junior partners. The status of the one *vis à vis* the other had not been closely defined. It was not so much, perhaps, that the relationship 'was rooted ... in ambiguity'[31] as that in a largely prescriptive age dependence was expressed through ceremony, attitudes, and behaviour rather than by written formulation. Such a relationship, as in all customary societies, could at any particular time be rapidly adjusted to the nuances of power and personal fortunes. Henry II soon indicated that he meant to introduce such an adjustment. For his part Malcolm IV of Scotland (1153–65) was shrewd enough to recognize that Henry meant business and that in those circumstances discretion was the better part of valour. From 1157 onwards a catalogue of deferential acts, albeit often veiled in ceremonies of companionship, was calculated to show that 'the Scots were meant to be seen in the role of obedient vassals'.[32] The Scottish king was required or invited (the distinction is largely academic) to appear before Henry II at Chester, to surrender Scottish pretensions to lands south of the rivers Esk and Tweed, to

[29] Stubbs (ed.), *Gesta Regis Henrici Secundi*, vol. 1, p. 92.
[30] *Calendar of the Gormanston Register* (as cited above, ch. 2, n. 17), pp. 9, 181.
[31] W. L. Warren, *Henry II* (London, 1973), p. 178.   [32] Barrow, *Kingship and Unity*, p. 47.

accompany the English king on one of his French campaigns, to hand over hostages to him and to attend the coronation of his son.

Henry II had given a chastening and blustering display of his power; and the Scottish kings had quaked in their shoes. Yet it is doubtful whether Henry's ambition *vis à vis* Scotland in these years amounted to more than a need for clear demonstrations of the loyalty and ultimate subservience of the king of Scotland. It was the folly, or bad luck, of William the Lion (1165–1214) to be captured by the English at Alnwick in July 1174 which gave Henry the opportunity to go much further. In the 'Treaty of Falaise' in that year he spelt out 'the categoric subjection of Scotland as a fief of the English crown'.[33] The public aspect of the humiliation reached its climax in the church of St Peter at York when King William, his brother, and the prelates and magnates of Scotland did homage and swore fealty to the king of England. It could indeed be argued that the Treaty of Falaise gave Henry II more than he wanted or at least could usefully manage. Within the ambit and the demands of his vast 'empire', the close supervision of matters Scottish hardly had a high priority. So it is no wonder that after 1175 'King Henry rode Scotland much more lightly than he need have done'.[34] Having neutralized the political threat that Scotland could be to England's northern border and having secured the unequivocal subservience of its king, Henry II was well content to rest on the laurels of his mastery (underwritten by the surrender of hostages and key castles) and to be satisfied with a social round of visits from the Scottish king whose amiability could not conceal their disciplinary force.

Much the same pattern was followed in Wales. There likewise from an early stage Henry II demonstrated clearly his twin ambitions – to recover lands and rights usurped during Stephen's reign (including those seized from Anglo-Norman barons) and to give his overlordship of Welsh princes a more precise and masterful content. His military expeditions into Wales in 1157, 1158, 1163 and 1165 were directed to those ends, not to the conquest of Wales or 'the destruction of all the Britons' (as the native chronicle averred). The military demonstrations were followed by the rituals of submission – parleys, pledges of good faith, the giving of hostages, and the payment of tribute. But as in Scotland, so in Wales Henry was intent on a closer definition of the nature of subjection. At Woodstock in July 1163 – on the very same occasion as Malcolm IV of Scotland made his submission – seven of the princes of Wales 'did homage to the king of the English and to Henry his son'. The Welsh clearly regarded this submission as more demeaning and threatening than their earlier client status, for the next year 'all the Welsh united to throw off the rule

[33] Stringer, *Earl David of Huntingdon*, p. 28. For a writ addressed by Henry II to his magnates and faithful men 'French, English and Scots of the whole of England and Scotland', see G. W. S. Barrow, 'A writ of Henry II for Dumfermline Abbey', *Scottish Historical Review*, 36 (1957), 138–43.
[34] Duncan, *Scotland*, p. 234.

of the French'.[35] Henry II may have forced the process of definition too rapidly and high-handedly in Wales and may have been over-ambitious there, at least in relation to the many calls on his time and resources. Nevertheless, the *modus vivendi* which he eventually seems to have reached with the Welsh princes gave him most of what he wanted: the position in Wales was stabilized (at least in so far as a measure of stability could be introduced into that turbulent country); Henry's overlordship was publicly acknowledged; the Marcher lords had been rapped over the knuckles; and the most powerful native prince, Lord Rhys (d. 1197), had agreed to act as the king's 'justice in the whole of Deheubarth'. Henry had reminded the Welsh princes forcefully of their client status and the limits of their power, both of which they might have been minded to overlook in Stephen's reign. He had thereby taught them and the Anglo-Norman barons of the March that Wales was firmly part of his dominions and that respect for his authority there was the beginning of political wisdom.

He repeated the same lesson in Ireland. Henry was not, of course, a party to the initial English invasion of Ireland; but once he was apprised of its success (and quite possibly also in response to an appeal from the native Irish) he quickly stepped in to impose the stamp of his own authority on the process of conquest and to claim the overlordship of the whole of Ireland, whether under English or native Gaelic control, for himself. Strongbow and his fellow *conquistadores* rushed to submit to him and so did most, if not quite all, of the native princes. His command, protection and patronage were henceforth key factors in English colony and native polities alike. The agreement he struck with the most powerful Gaelic king, Ruaidrí Ó Conchobair of Connacht, in 1175, the so-called 'Treaty of Windsor', acknowledged as much. Like the 'Treaty of Falaise' with the king of Scotland a year earlier, it was a formal and written acknowledgement of Henry's senior status and overlordship. The 'Treaty' proved to be short-lived; but in a few years Henry II had established unequivocally, for himself and his successors, that Ireland lay within the power and authority of the kings of England. The fabric of the king's authority in Ireland may have been very different from that in England, and most of the momentum of political life may have lain with English lords and Gaelic leaders; but the ultimate authority of the king of England as 'lord of Ireland' (*dominus Hibernie*) was never henceforth called in question.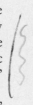

It would be an exaggeration, of course, to claim that Henry II had a 'policy' for the British Isles. His attitude towards Ireland, Scotland and Wales was determined by the general needs and priorities of his 'empire'; so was the time, attention and resources he could devote to them. His policies in these countries were very much of a piece with those he pursued elsewhere, notably the recovery of his rights and the closer definition and imposition of his

[35] Ralph de Diceto, *Opera Historica* (as cited above, ch. 1, n. 49), vol. 1, p. 311; *Brut*, p. 63.

superiority. More often than not he seems to have responded to challenges and opportunities rather than worked to a preordained plan. That, however, is not to deny that his policies in Wales, Scotland and Ireland were informed by a common purpose. During his stays in England, he often dealt with their problems together: the king of Scots and the Welsh princes were summoned together to Woodstock in 1163, while in 1177 the problems of Wales and Ireland were considered simultaneously at Oxford. Conditions and opportunities in the three countries were, of course, very different; but Henry's ambition in all of them – especially as it was realized between 1174 and 1177 – was basically similar – to impose or create a stable political order (or, in Wales and Ireland, as stable an order as the quicksilver habits of native polities and Anglo-Norman barons allowed) and to secure as precise an acknowledgement of his superiority as was possible. Viewed in this light his achievements, amid the crowded concerns of a busy reign, were quite exceptional, more exceptional than is, perhaps, sometimes realized. He led the first royal expedition into Wales for over thirty years, and after his last expedition there in 1165 it was to be almost fifty years before a king of England entered the country. His one expedition to Ireland brought that country firmly within the ambit of his dominions; there was to be no successor to it for almost forty years. In Scotland he was able to extract an unprecedented formal acknowledgement of the subjection of the kingdom to England; Scotland after the 'Treaty of Falaise' was, theoretically at least, a satellite and client state.

Throughout the British Isles he had greatly intensified the authority of the English monarchy. He had not aimed at the military conquest of the outlying regions of Britain, though some of his expeditions (notably those of 1165 to Wales and of 1171–2 to Ireland) showed that he commanded a formidable military machine against which native opposition was helpless. What he had done was to demonstrate the awesome military might of the English monarchy and its ability to achieve an overlordship of all the British Isles commensurate with his needs. It was Gerald of Wales who best recognized the scope of his achievement:

Crossing the deep sea, he visited Ireland with a fleet, and gloriously subdued it; Scotland also he vanquished, capturing its king, William . . . He remarkably extended the kingdom's limits and boundaries [until they reached] from the ocean on the south to the Orkney islands in the north. With his powerful grasp he included the whole island of Britain in one monarchy, even as it is enclosed by the sea.[36]

Gerald was by no means always fulsome in his comments on Henry II. But on this occasion he was generous enough to recognize that Henry had secured a domination of the whole of the British Isles such as none of his predecessors had enjoyed, and had stamped (or restamped) the authority of the king firmly

[36] Gerald of Wales, *Opera*, ed. J. S. Brewer *et al*. Rolls Series (8 vols., London, 1861–91), vol. VIII, p. 156.

on the process whereby the outlying parts of the British Isles were brought, in greater or lesser degree, under English control.

In this respect at least King John proved to be a worthy son of his father. As with Henry, so with John his attitude towards Scotland, Ireland and Wales was only part – and a small part at that – of his policies and ambitions for his dominions as a whole, notably the assertion and defence of his political authority and, after 1204, the recovery of his northern French lands. Even so, his reign revealed once more the frightening power that lay at the command of the English king and his ability, should he be so minded, to convert his overlordship of the British Isles into a much more demanding and even suffocating domination.

In Wales the tactics of control and submission of earlier days were certainly cleverly pursued and exploited; but menacing innovations were also introduced.[37] Relationships between the king of England and Welsh princes were now, for the first time as far as we know, formally committed to writing, and charters of submission were exacted. This represented a palpable advance in the powers of overlordship. It defined in writing – and in documents deposited in the king of England's treasury – relationships which had hitherto been oral and customary; and it defined them (along with the penalties for any breach thereof) in a terminology of whose meaning the king was the ultimate interpreter and arbiter. The powers of overlordship were also increasingly itemized and thereby intensified. There was talk of tenurial as well as of personal dependence, of military obligations and annual renders, of judicial answerability in the king's court, and of the overriding fealty of the greater subjects of the Welsh princelings to the king of England. Through custodies, forfeiture and conquest John had a far greater territorial stake in Wales than any previous English king, even Henry I. If anyone was in doubt about his power there, the two military expeditions of 1211 surely put paid to those doubts. They penetrated further into north Wales than any earlier royal expedition; they reduced the most powerful Welsh prince of the day, Llywelyn ab Iorwerth (d. 1240) of Gwynedd, to the most abject surrender; and they gave the king direct control of vast areas of north-east and west Wales. In short, they were devastating. In their military thoroughness (reflected again in the aborted campaign of 1212) they showed that conquest, 'a lasting solution of the Welsh problem',[38] was well within the king of England's reach. Much of John's achievement in Wales was to be undone during the last four years of his reign; but he had shown clearly how English overlordship could be intensified there, how the English crown could become the central force in the domi-

---

[37] See in general Lloyd, *History of Wales*, vol. II, pp. 612–23, 631–50; Davies, *Conquest*, pp. 292–7; and the seminal article by J. B. Smith, 'Magna Carta and the Charters of the Welsh Princes', *English Historical Review*, 99 (1984), pp. 344–62.
[38] J. B. Smith, 'Magna Carta and the Charters of the Welsh Princes', 356.

nation of the country and what diplomatic, judicial and military means were readily to hand to effect that domination.

His achievements in Ireland were equally remarkable.[39] In spite of the fact that he had been lord of Ireland since childhood and had visited the lordship in 1185, there is no reason to believe that John as king regarded the country as other than a source for money and resources to be used for the promotion of his ambitions elsewhere. Yet he left the impress of English royal authority more firmly on Ireland than, arguably, any other medieval king, his father included. He kept a careful eye on its affairs, especially for signs of disaffection and over-ambition among his English barons there, if only to ensure that their quarrels and ambitions did not threaten his authority or that political malcontents did not export their conspiracies from his court to Ireland, or vice-versa. He alternatively cajoled and browbeat native Gaelic rulers, ensnaring several of them in the tentacles of a novel feudal dependence. As in Wales, so in Ireland John's reign witnessed a momentous advance in the king's territorial stake in the lordship, notably through a series of custodies and dramatic forfeitures and by the construction of key castles, such as Dublin and Athlone. In Ireland, unlike Wales, the royal presence was also advanced in his reign by the deliberate transplant of a governmental and legal structure which was monarchical in its assumptions and modelled closely on English royal practice. But the most striking manifestation of royal power was, of course, John's whirlwind Irish expedition of 1210. It was as decisive in its impact as his father's had been in 1171–2: it crushed opponents (such as Hugh de Lacy) utterly; it taught doubters and waverers (such as William Marshal) a sobering lesson; and it gave the native Irish kings an opportunity to display their loyalty and military support.

Historians have varied widely in their views on John's actions in Ireland. To G. H. Orpen, those actions 'seem to have been swayed by capricious favouritism or by vindictive personal animosity, without any regard for the general weal of his Irish dominion'.[40] W. L. Warren, on the other hand, is impressed by the 'constantly . . . close attention' John gave to Irish affairs and by the 'astonishing and impressive strategic grasp' which informed his 'plan' for the country; he was 'the most successful high king Ireland had ever seen'.[41] It may be that there is some truth in both arguments. It can hardly be doubted that many of John's actions in Ireland were prompted by the needs of the political moment, whether to reward a favourite or to destroy an opponent. But equally the frequency and high-handedness of his actions betokened a determination to bring, or rather to keep, Ireland firmly under his control and

[39] Apart from general works, reference may be made in particular to Empey, 'Settlement of the Kingdom of Limerick'; Warren, 'King John and Ireland'; W. L. Warren, 'The Historian as Private Eye', *Historical Studies*, 9 (1974), pp. 1–18; and P. A. Brand, 'Ireland and the literature of the early common law', *Irish Jurist*, new series 16 (1981), pp. 95–113.

[40] Orpen, *Ireland under the Normans*, vol. ii, p. 320.

[41] Warren, 'King John and Ireland', pp. 27–8, 39.

to impose the stamp of royal authority, patronage, governance and law on it, or at least on English Ireland. At the very least it can hardly be denied that his reign 'saw a greater degree of royal involvement in Ireland than almost any other period during the middle ages'.[42]

John had flexed the muscles of his power in Ireland in 1210, in Wales in 1211. He had already done so in Scotland in 1209.[43] Scotland was, of course, in a different league from Wales and Ireland. Whereas the latter two were part of the king of England's dominions, Scotland was, and was recognized to be, a separate kingdom with its own independent monarchy. Nevertheless, if the Scottish king overstepped the mark and showed an unacceptable and threatening degree of independence, then a sharp rap over the knuckles could serve to remind him of his junior status *vis à vis* the king of England. John delivered such a rap to the ageing William the Lion in 1209. The sight of an English castle being built at Tweedmouth, opposite Berwick, and of the ranks of a large English army being assembled were enough to chasten William the Lion into speedy submission. The terms of the accord concluded between William and John at Norham in August 1209 and subsequently confirmed and extended in February 1212 are not fully known; but that they involved a fairly comprehensive humiliation – including the surrender of hostages, the imposition of a large fine, the handing over of the king of Scotland's daughters to John to be married, and a concession that John should also arrange the marriage of William the Lion's heir – is not open to doubt. It may be claimed that theoretically 'the judicial position of the king and kingdom (of Scotland) remained unchanged' as a result of these agreements; but in terms of the realities of power John had surely 'behaved as though he were suzerain of Scotland'.[44]

John's achievements in Scotland, Wales and Ireland especially in the years 1209–12 proved short-lived; they were soon overturned by the consequences of his own political folly and military defeat. It is doubtful, indeed, whether he had the wish or the means to build a more permanent structure of royal authority on the basis of the great demonstrations of power which he had given in the three countries; his mind and ambitions were elsewhere. Yet his achievement was very real: he had shown that the 'super-overlordship' of the British Isles was no pipe-dream;[45] he had given a terrifying glimpse of the power of the English king's governmental and military machine; he had underlined the basic lesson that in the domination of the British Isles as in the governance of the kingdom of England the role of the king of England was central. Contemporaries stood in awe of his achievement: 'the king', said the Tewkesbury annalist, 'subjugated the whole of Ireland and the greater part of

[42] Frame, *Colonial Ireland*, p. 53.
[43] The fullest recent review is in Duncan, *Scotland*, pp. 240–55.
[44] Duncan, *Scotland*, p. 249; Stringer, *Earl David*, p. 47.
[45] The phrase is borrowed from Barrow, *Bruce*, p. 11.

Wales to his authority'.[46] The Barnwell chronicler was even more impressed: 'There is now no one in Ireland, Scotland and Wales who does not obey the command of the king of England; that, as is well known, is more than any of his ancestors had achieved.'[47] English domination of the British Isles seemed now to be truly at hand.

Whether the king of England chose to exercise and intensify such domination depended very considerably on political circumstances in England and on the king's preoccupations elsewhere. During much of his long reign Henry III was too enfeebled politically or too concerned with his European dreams and other priorities to attend closely to the domination of the outlying parts of the British Isles. But during the 1240s and 1250s in particular – in other words at the very period that he was beginning to come to terms with the permanent loss of his northern French dominions – he and his advisers showed that earlier lessons and pretensions had not been forgotten. It was then, as the Welsh chronicler put it pregnantly, that 'the English remembered their old ways'.[48]

The chronicler had a particular reason for his statement: it was Wales which was the prime target of Henry III's 'British' ambitions in these years.[49] Its political fragmentation and geographical proximity made it an easy target, while the death in 1240 of Llywelyn the Great of Gwynedd at long last cleared the field for Henry III to pursue his ambitions. He seized his opportunity with both hands; and within the next fifteen years Wales, in Matthew Paris' phrase, 'was brought to nought'.[50] The feudal noose was placed more securely than ever before round the throats of the native Welsh princelings. Their lands were to be held 'in chief' of the king of England and by his gift; they were required to receive and act on all royal mandates; they were to bring their disputes to his court to be settled at his discretion. The king of England made it amply clear that he would tolerate no alternative or intermediate claim to native overlordship in Wales; he and he alone was the ultimate lord of all Welshmen or, as he put it in the feudal formulae of the day, 'the homages and services of all the barons and nobles of Wales shall remain to the king and his heirs in perpetuity'.[51] Finally, in case the message of their own relative impotence had not been fully understood by the Welsh princelings (especially the prince of Gwynedd), Henry III added two chilling threats: total confiscation of their lands would be the penalty for any breach of their oath to the king of England, while failure to produce legitimate heirs of their bodies would likewise lead to the reversion of their lands to the English crown.

It was a sustained and remorseless exercise in the pulverization of the power

---

46 *Annales Monastici* (as cited above, ch. 1, n. 23), vol. 1, p. 59.
47 Stubbs, *Memoriale Fratris Walteri de Coventria* (as cited above, ch. 1, n. 57), vol. 11, p. 203.
48 *Brut*, p. 105.
49 The most detailed recent discussion is in J. B. Smith, *Llywelyn ap Gruffudd*, pp. 29–81. See also Davies, *Conquest*, pp. 300–7.
50 Matthew Paris, *Chronica Majora*, vol. 1V, p. 647.
51 *Litt. Wallie*, p. 8 and the classic exposition in the introduction pp. xxxviii-l.

and status of the native Welsh polities. It was accompanied by other indications that the king of England had now seized the initiative in Wales, not only from native Welsh dynasts but from the Marcher lords also. Between 1240 and 1250 the king's territorial presence in Wales was dramatically increased through conquest, reversion and manipulation. Two impressive stone castles of great strength were built at a huge cost in Diserth and Degannwy in north-east Wales, and other royal castles in the country were refurbished. Two royal campaigns against north Wales in 1241 and 1245–6 showed twice within a few years that Henry III, like his father before him, had the military means to reduce the prince of Gwynedd to his knees. Even the Marcher lords were reminded in these years that the king's authority could be intruded into their affairs in a variety of ways. Arguably for the first time since the coming of the Normans, the king of England now dominated the affairs of Wales in a sustained and regular fashion; he would henceforth set the pace for the advance of English power there and would continue to do so until the final conquest. Furthermore there were signs that the shift in attitude and orientation was now to be a permanent one. Already in 1247 the county of Chester and the castles of Diserth and Degannwy had been made appurtenant to the Crown in perpetuity; in 1254, when the Lord Edward was granted Chester and all the lands then held by the king in Wales, a crucial stipulation was added that they 'should never be separated from the Crown but should remain entirely to the kings of England for ever'.[52] The interest of the king of England in Wales had now, as it were, been permanently institutionalized; it was henceforth not to be spasmodic nor the responsibility of a cadet branch of the royal family; it was one of the obligations that attached to the Crown itself.

The transformation in the rôle of the king in the affairs of Ireland in the mid-thirteenth century is by no means as dramatic or obvious as it was in Wales, in good part because the circumstances and chronology of the conquest of Ireland had given the English monarchy a much greater territorial, governmental and institutional rôle in Ireland *ab initio* than it enjoyed in Wales. Nevertheless, some of the circumstances that had brought the Crown much more into the forefront of affairs in Wales prevailed in Ireland also. In particular the fragmentation of both Meath and Leinster after the deaths of Walter de Lacy (1241) and Anselm Marshal (1245) without direct male heirs weakened two of the great aristocratic supremacies. Furthermore the earldom of Ulster came into the Crown's hands after the death of Hugh de Lacy (1242) and was to be retained by the king or his son until 1263, while the extensive de Burgh lands in Tipperary and Connacht were in Crown custody 1243–50. Within a very short period the balance of territorial power in

---

[52] *Calendar of Patent Rolls 1232–47*, p. 501; T. Rymer (ed.), *Foedera*, revised edn. (4 vols., London, 1816–69), vol. I, part 2, p. 297.

Ireland had 'quickly altered'.[53] The Crown seemed, temporarily or otherwise, to occupy a higher profile in Ireland and that at the very time when the momentum of the English aristocratic drive in the country seemed to be faltering and when there were signs of what has been termed a 'Gaelic resurgence'. And in 1254 when Ireland was granted to the Lord Edward it was stipulated, as with the conquered lands in Wales, that 'the land of Ireland shall never be separated from the crown of England'.

The relationship with Scotland was of its nature different. Scotland was a kingdom whose independence, though the subject of private and even occasionally public reservations, was not challenged by the English king. For most of the years 1217–96, relations between the two monarchies were good, even at times cordial. Proprieties were observed; marriage agreements concluded; and treaties (especially the Treaty of York, 1237) arranged to defuse sources of tensions. Good relations and diplomatic niceties, however, are only part of the story. In truth the kings of England 'did not always behave as though they recognized the political independence of Scotland'.[54] They pulled every diplomatic wire at the papal court to ensure that the Scottish request for the rite of anointing for their kings was not granted; they cheekily claimed that the king of England had the right to a share of the crusading taxes from Scotland as from his own dominions; they dropped hints (as in 1253) that good relations involved the expectation of 'aid and counsel' (including military assistance) for the king of England's foreign enterprises; they used marriage alliances into the Scottish royal family as routes for influence and supervision as well as good relations, and also, very pointedly in 1244, as a way of forestalling any unwelcome French marital alliances by the Scots. They had the good taste and the good sense not to press the issue of the feudal subjection of Scotland to England too often; but they could not resist the temptation to remind the Pope of it (as in 1235) or to raise it at an embarrassing occasion (such as the marriage of Alexander III and Margaret of England at York at Christmas 1251).

It was in the middle decades of the thirteenth century – the very period which, as we have seen, was crucial in the assertion of royal power in Wales and Ireland – that the king of England was provided with an opportunity to remind the Scots that he was, at the very least, the senior partner in their relationship and therefore expected from them some of the deference that junior status involves. As in Wales, so in Scotland the immediate pretext and opportunity for the English king to throw his weight around arose from the tensions of domestic politics – notably factional disagreements among the

---

53 Otway-Ruthven, *Ireland*, pp. 100–1, 191; *NHI*, vol. II, p. 241; Frame, 'Ireland and the Barons' War', 160.
54 Barrow, *Bruce*, p. 11. Cf. Barrow, *Kingship and Unity*, p. 150: 'Neither the crown nor the baronage of England ... saw any need or justification for the survival of Scotland as an independent realm'.

Scottish political community and, after 1249, the almost inevitable turmoil of a minority rule. But neighbours who interfere are normally those who believe they have the duty, right and power to do so; the opportunity only provides the occasion. Henry III was such a neighbour. In 1244 and again in 1255 he brought armies to the Scottish border (as his father had done); twice he imposed agreements which seemed in practice, whatever the theoretical protestations, to compromise Scottish political independence seriously. It may be that Henry III's actions in these years can, and should, be seen merely as those of a meddlesome neighbour and over-anxious father-in-law.[55] Yet one contemporary observer was worried that his tutelage over Scottish affairs 'might result in the dishonour of the king and kingdom' (of Scotland); and modern historians have been prompted to wonder whether he 'regarded the government (of Scotland) as being subject to his overriding authority'.[56] An interfering neighbour in one generation, however honourable his motives, might appear as 'superior lord' in the next.

'King Henry (III)'s supervision of Scottish affairs', so Sir Maurice Powicke suggested, '. . . anticipated in some respects the situation in 1286 after the death of Alexander III. It would live in the memory of the young Edward [I].'[57] To suggest as much is to suggest that there was, perhaps, more continuity and conscious recollection in the policies of the English king towards Scotland, and quite possibly Wales and Ireland, than is normally conceded. Were the episodes of the assertion and intensification of royal authority over the outlying parts of the British Isles under Henry II, John and Henry III discussed above more than separate, discrete incidents? Were they informed by a common ambition and direction, which emerged whenever the opportunity presented itself? The evidence is not altogether lacking for such a view. In Wales in 1240 Henry III's advisers declared it their intention to restore the *status quo* that had prevailed in John's reign, presumably at the high point of English power in 1211–12.[58] Edward I's advisers likewise looked back self-consciously to the past. In Wales they culled judicial precedents from the years 1247 to 1258 – the very years when English royal power was at its zenith – to support their case for royal judicial supervision of Welsh affairs. Likewise when the royal clerks were commissioned to compile a working dossier of Welsh documents, it was 1240 once more which they took in effect as their *terminus a quo*.[59] When Edward set about asserting his supremacy over Scotland in the 1290s he ordered the monastic houses of England and his own

---

[55] Such in particular is A. A. M. Duncan's view, *Scotland*, pp. 535–7, 560–77.
[56] Melrose chronicle in Anderson, *Sources of Scottish History*, vol. II, p. 583; Alan Young, 'The Political Role of Walter Comyn, Earl of Menteith, during the Minority of Alexander III of Scotland' in K. J. Stringer (ed.), *The Nobility of Medieval Scotland*, 136–7.
[57] F. M. Powicke, *The Thirteenth Century 1216–1307* (Oxford, 1953), p. 592.
[58] *Litt. Wallie*, p. 9.
[59] J. Conway Davies (ed.), *The Welsh Assize Roll 1277–84* (Cardiff, 1940), pp. 13–28; *Litt. Wallie*.

clerks to rummage through their chronicles and records and provide every scrap of supporting evidence they could lay hands on. The past was vigorously called into service to promote the claim of the kings of England to domination over the British Isles. To that extent it may not be mistaken to detect continuities and even conscious imitation in their policies.

Yet we must beware of importing a Whiggish interpretation into our view of English domination of the British Isles and notably of royal policy. Some periods in which English royal power over Wales, Ireland and Scotland was intensified to an unusual degree can, perhaps, be identified; and it may not be altogether fanciful to suggest, as is done above, that intensification in one area is likely to be accompanied by intensification in another. But such periods of intensification cannot be plotted on some cumulative graph of royal power leading inexorably towards eventual conquest. Intensification of royal authority and involvement in Wales, Ireland and (in a different form) Scotland was often but one facet of a general assertion of monarchical authority and, as in the case of Henry II and John, was subsidiary to more important concerns elsewhere and preparatory to the effective pursuit of those concerns. Kings seized their opportunities as they arose, as in Scotland in 1174/5 or in Wales in 1240, rather than working to any premeditated plan. Comparisons between Wales, Ireland and Scotland may be instructive, but they are in a sense artificial, since it is the contrasts between them and between the relationships of the English crown and each of them which are often most striking. In particular relationships with Scotland were those between two kingdoms, whereas Wales and Ireland were clearly regarded as part of the king of England's dominions. Similarities there certainly are between royal policy in Wales and in Ireland: in both countries the Crown had to deal with native polities and with a powerful English immigrant aristocracy. But the differences in the nature of the problems confronting the Crown in the two countries and in the institutional position of the king within the structure of power in the two countries are quite as striking as are the similarities.

To that extent it is misleading to talk of a single policy or attitude on the part of the English crown towards the outlying countries of the British Isles or to detect sinister and far-reaching implications in every assertion of power by the king of England in Ireland, Scotland and Wales. Yet it cannot be denied that the power and attitude of the king of England was central, in one way or another, to the story of the Anglo-Norman and English domination of the British Isles. It could hardly be otherwise in a polity which was so monar-chically-dominated as that of medieval England. Every king of England from William the Conqueror to Edward I (with the exception of Stephen and Richard) left his imprint on Wales, Scotland and, after 1170, Ireland. Some left a stronger imprint than others; some seemed more reluctant to take a direct role than others; from the thirteenth century, with the loss of the northern French lands, royal interest and involvement in all three countries appear to be greater and more sustained. All of them assumed – though it was an assumption more taken for granted than openly expressed – that the ultimate domination of the British Isles was naturally and rightfully theirs, even if it was only spasmodically (in the 1170s, from 1209 to 1212, or in the 1240s and 1250s) that they showed what they could, if they so wished, make of the claim. Much of the groundwork of domination and settlement was left to the aristocracy; but ultimately the role of the king was central to the process. Once he came to occupy a higher profile in the process of domination, especially from the thirteenth century, it could be argued that domination would sooner or later lead to conquest. That conquest would be a royal conquest.

5

The intensification of lordship

In much of Wales and Ireland, the Anglo-Norman conquerors were initially often well content with the acknowledgement of their overlordship by native rulers and communities. In truth, they had little alternative. Novel as their tactics and equipment might have been, they did not have the military means to establish a permanent presence in any depth. In both Wales and Ireland, intensive alien colonization, which alone could underpin a conquest in depth, was restricted to a few enclaves, generally confined to the lowlands and coastal districts and frequently isolated from each other. Beyond these enclaves lay frontier districts, or marchlands, into which alien systems of control and governance were beginning to penetrate hesitatingly. Beyond these marchlands in turn lay native districts – Welshries as they would be called in Wales from the thirteenth century onwards – where effective alien authority was spasmodic in its impact and often nominal in character and where social customs, law and the framework of governance and control remained native and largely in native hands.

It is often only in the fourteenth century that the nature of English lordship in Wales and Ireland begins to come fully into documentary view; but the evidence of the extents and accounts of that period reflects a pattern of authority which was already generations old. Two examples may serve to illustrate the nature of that authority. Brecon was one of the oldest and richest of Anglo-Norman lordships in Wales.[1] The Normans had arrived there by the 1090s, built castles to assert their authority, subinfeudated estates to the lord's vassals, established boroughs and founded manors in the lowlands of the Usk and Llynfi valleys. English-speaking colonists migrated in some numbers in the area, as the place-, personal- and field-names of the early evidence make clear. Individuals and communities contiguous with these English and Anglicized settlements were gradually brought into a rent-paying relationship with the new lords of Brecon. Sometimes indeed we can catch a glimpse of such a relationship being forged in the fourteenth century: thus in 1341, 186 men from

---

[1] W. Rees, 'The Medieval Lordship of Brecon', *Transactions of the Honourable Society of Cymmrodorion*, 1915–16, pp. 165–224; Davies, *Lordship and Society in the March of Wales*, pp. 91–5, 101–3.

Cwmwd Commos attorned to the lord of Brecon for their services and gave him a gift of £100 as a token of their new relationship with him. Over most of the lordship of Brecon, however, the native Welsh were still organized as self-regulating, self-governing communities whose formal links with the lord of Brecon were tenuous and occasional. Thus, to give one example, an inquisition of 1298 declared that the three hundred Welshmen of Cantref Tewdos owed the lord suit of court once a month, an annual fee-farm for the right to pasture their animals, a tribute of sixty cows every other year, and unspecified military service.[2] That was all. The lord was in no sense their land-lord; their land was allodial, its descent and distribution being governed by their own customs. The degree of seignorial governance was minimal; the collection of renders was the affair of the community itself, whose proctors acted as intermediaries with the lord.

Much the same sort of pattern is reflected in Ireland in the great Butler lordship covering much of northern county Tipperary. In the central plain around Thurles there had been rapid and intensive colonial settlement. Manors and boroughs were founded; land was intensively exploited for tillage; Irish tenants were absorbed into a manorial framework; and fiefs were even created for Irish leaders (such as the fief of Clochan held by the Ó Ceinnéidigh (O'Kennedy) by service of one knight and suit at the court at Nenagh). But as one progressed north-west, the 'colonial settlement became progressively thinner' and 'the northern septs', such as the Ó Ceinnéidigh and Ó Cearbaill (O'Carroll), 'retained a wide measure of autonomy'.[3] In the fourteenth century, and doubtless earlier, the Butlers were negotiating with the leaders of these groups on terms which clearly conceded the autonomy which they enjoyed, even if they also sought to clarify their obligations.[4]

Brecon and Tipperary are but two examples of the way in which English lordship in Wales and Ireland had to adjust to the limits of its own effective authority and to the realities of the social situation which confronted it. In these circumstances what the English lords – king and aristocrats alike – wanted, at least initially, was the formal acknowledgement of their *superioritas* over native society and its leaders and the establishment of basic ground rules for regulating the relationships between them. So it was that Lord Rhys of Deheubarth acknowledged the superiority of Henry in 1171–2 and accepted from him the post of justiciar of south Wales, with its clear connotations of delegated governmental authority; so likewise the powerful Ruaidrí Ó Conchobair, through his emissaries, acknowledged in 1175 that he was king 'under' Henry II. A similar pattern of acknowledgement operated at aristocratic level: in 1269 Áed Buide Ó Néill of Tír Eóghain recognized that he held his kingship

---

[2] *Cal. Inquisitions Post Mortem*, vol. III, no. 552.
[3] Empey, 'The Norman Period' in Nolan (ed.), *Tipperary* (as cited above, ch. 2, n. 47), pp. 71–91. The quotations are from pp. 86–87.
[4] Curtis (ed.), *Calendar of Ormond Deeds*, vol. I, no. 682; vol. II, nos. 34, 46.

(*regalitas*) from 'his lord', Walter de Burgh, earl of Ulster; while later in the century Ralph Pipard of Ardee (co. Louth) granted to Aonghus Mac Mathgamna (MacMahon) the kingship (*regalitas*) of his land of Cremourne.⁵ The terminology of authority within native Irish society changed in the later middle ages, but when the earl of Kildare nominated (or more likely confirmed) an Ó Ceallaigh (O'Kelly) as 'captain of his nation', he was in reality continuing the same tradition of king-making.⁶ Native princes were being confirmed in their positions, but now as dependants of a foreign over-king rather than of a native one.

What did such acknowledgement of superiority entail? In truth, often very little. No territorial bond had been established; no specified military service, other than the pre-existing obligation of hosting, was exacted. How minimal the obligations might be is indicated by the fact that the sole recorded due payable by the native lord of the commote of Senghennydd to the Clare lord of Glamorgan was a heriot of a horse and arms on his death. Nor was there a clearly-defined code to specify what was entailed in the acceptance of overlordship. Thus, when the king of Connacht acknowledged his dependence on the earl of Ulster in 1324 all that was stipulated was that he was 'to behave according to the best behaviour of his father, Áed' (*sicut aliquo tempore Odo pater noster melius gerere consuevit*). That would have been a hopelessly vague obligation in the eyes of a contemporary English lawyer.⁷

There were, it is true, a range of mechanisms for maintaining and enforcing relationships once entered into with native rulers and communities.⁸ Hostages were surrendered as a guarantee of continuing good behaviour; tributes might be exacted, whether at the initial submission or on a more regular basis; military service in the suzerain's army was required, as the most practical and public display of deference in a warrior society; periodic attendance at court, both in a social and judicial sense, might be expected. Superiority also entailed accepting the disciplinary powers of the overlord. Fines were imposed on client rulers who offended the overlord: two of the princelings of the uplands of mid-Wales were only able to buy their way back into Henry II's favour in 1175 by offering to pay a composition fine of one thousand head of cattle each, and the earliest surviving Irish Pipe Roll of 1211–12 makes it clear that similar fines were likewise imposed on Irish kings to keep them on the straight and

⁵ *H.M.C. De L'Isle and Dudley Mss.* (as cited above, ch.3, n. 28), vol. I, pp. 32–3; K. Sims in *Seanchas Ard Mhacha* 9 (1978–9), 87.
⁶ G. Mac Niocaill (ed.), *The Red Book of the Earls of Kildare*, Irish Manuscripts Commission (Dublin, 1964), p. 154.
⁷ G. T. Clark (ed.), *Cartae et Alia Munimenta . . . de Glamorgancia*, 2nd edn. (6 vols., Cardiff, 1910), vol. II, p. 661; *H.M.C. De L'Isle and Dudley Mss.*, vol. I, p. 32. There is an excellent analysis of the situation in Glamorgan by J. B. Smith in Pugh (ed.), *Glamorgan County History*, vol. III, chap. 2.
⁸ Cf. above pp. 57–8.

narrow path of obedience.⁹ Client rulers were also expected to keep their own dependants in order: Henry II laid on Ruaidrí Ó Conchobair in 1175 the duty to discipline (*justiciare*) those under him, while later agreements make 'captains of nations' responsible for the misdeeds of the men of their 'nation'.¹⁰ Finally, of course, the power of an overlord (be he king or aristocrat) included the right to depose a recalcitrant or ineffective client chieftain and to establish an alternative candidate in his place. This right was specifically spelt out in the Ó Néill–de Burgh agreement of 1269: the earl reserved the right to 'expel me [Ó Néill] from the kingship which I ought to hold of him, without hope of securing grace or mercy, and to bestow it on whomsoever he wished'. Nor was this merely a theoretical right, as the native annals make abundantly clear; the vicious segmentary politics of native society gave the Anglo-Normans ample opportunity to exercise it.¹¹

The powers of overlordship were, therefore, less insubstantial and more interventionist than first impressions might suggest. Yet those powers were at best occasional and irregular in their impact; their force and effectiveness depended much more than did the powers of lordship elsewhere on the character of the lord, the seizing of opportunities, and the periodic display of military power. Such overlordship was, of its very nature, precarious. Native leaders surrendered as little of their authority as they could: when Áed Ó Néill came to pay his respects to King John in 1210 he studiously avoided giving hostages, the true mark of submission (according to the Annals of Inisfallen).¹² Submissions exacted from such men were fragile in the extreme; they rarely outlasted the convenience of either party, especially that of the native ruler. Anglo-Norman commentators declared themselves regularly outraged by the duplicity and fickleness of the Welsh and the Irish in this respect; they termed it variously lightheadedness (*levitas cervicosa*) or treachery, and attributed it to a deep-seated national character-weakness. 'The shameless act of perjury' (as Gerald of Wales called it) of Domnall Mór Ó Briain, king of Thomond (d. 1194), may serve to illustrate this 'weakness' and to reveal the fragility of overlordship. Domnall accepted the custody of the city of Limerick from the king of England in 1176; agreed to surrender it at the king's command; and underwrote his promise by swearing solemn oaths and surrendering hostages. But once the English had withdrawn, he promptly broke his word. 'The treacherous Domnall', so remarked Gerald with all the moral indignation at his command, 'showed the kind of confidence we must henceforth place in the pledged word of the

---

⁹ Lloyd, *History of Wales*, vol. II, p. 546; O. Davies and D. B. Quinn (eds.), *Irish Pipe Roll of 14 John*, Ulster Journal of Archaeology, supplement (Belfast, 1941), pp. 36–7.
¹⁰ Mac Niocaill (ed.), *Red Book of Earls of Kildare*, p. 129.
¹¹ See, for example, *Annals of Connacht*, pp.185, 189.
¹² Mac Airt (ed.), *Annals of Inisfallen*, p. 339.

Irish.'[13] The truth was, of course, more complex than such moral certainties might suggest. One man's opportunity was another man's treachery. Nor were the Anglo-Normans themselves unwilling to act on that principle when it suited them (as indeed the Welsh chronicler remarked bitterly in his account of an infamous massacre of Welshmen at Abergavenny in 1175).[14] More importantly, charges of faithlessness concealed the fact that the acts and language of submission meant different things in different societies. To native princelings, long habituated to the remarkable fluidity of supremacies in native politics, submission represented no more than an acceptance of the realities of power of the present moment, a trimming of the sails to the prevailing wind. To Anglo-Norman barons, familiar with a much closer, king-centred chain of command and discipline and long used to the rituals and terminology of dependence which expected life-long subjection, submission and lordship had very different connotations. Where perceptions and assumptions were so far apart and where the structure of 'political' relationships was so very different, it was very difficult to establish an acceptable pattern of overlordship.

Political realities played further havoc with such prospects. Even when subjection was acknowledged, the overlord had often to work hard to keep his client princelings in order, spending time, effort and money in 'drawing' them 'into the royal peace'.[15] Even such efforts might not be enough when native power was resurgent. Thus during the principate of Llywelyn the Great of Gwynedd and again in the 1250s and 1260s the minor princelings of south and central Wales deserted the overlordship of the king of England and the Marcher lords for that of the prince of Gwynedd. In much the same fashion, so it was reported to the English government in 1259, Brian Ó Néill 'presumptuously bears himself as king of the kings of Ireland' and thus sought to attract to himself the overlordship of native Ireland.[16] Such assertive native overlordship was not afraid of baring the teeth of its power in order to get its way: when Llywelyn ab Iorwerth was attempting to draw the local leaders of the upper Wye valley into the orbit of his influence in the 1230s his constable warned those who sought to frustrate his ambition that they 'will be choosing war and will certainly have war'.[17] Nor were these empty words: 'sometimes', as a judicial record has it, territory, and thereby lordship, might 'by fortune of war pass into Welsh hands'.[18] That indeed frequently happened in Wales in the twelfth and thirteenth centuries, and in Ireland in the later middle ages. To give but two examples from south-east Wales: in the early 1170s much of Gwent Iscoed was overrun by the Welsh and even the castle of Caerleon was briefly captured; in the 1180s there was a similar Welsh backlash in the lordship of Glamorgan (after the

---

13 *Expugnatio*, pp. 166–7 (Bk 2, ch. 14).   14 *Brut*, p. 71.   15 *CDI*, vol. 1, p. 273.
16 *Close Rolls 1259–61*, p. 64.   17 *Anc. Corr. conc. Wales*, pp. 35–6, 53.
18 J. Conway Davies, *Welsh Assize Roll* (as cited above, ch. 4, n. 59), 291.

death of Earl William of Gloucester in 1183) in which Cardiff and Kenfig were burnt. Such attacks were almost annual in their occurrence in much of Wales and Ireland. It is normal, and natural, to plot such attacks on a narrative of Anglo-Welsh and Anglo-Irish relations and to speak of a Welsh advance or of Gaelic revival. But in a world in which the total expulsion of English lordship and English settlers could not realistically be contemplated, it is perhaps more meaningful to construe such raids and counter-raids as attempts to change or redress the balance of power and overlordship and to qualify, contain and limit the claims of English kings and aristocrats to superiority over native society and dynasties. Likewise the struggle between the princes of Gwynedd and the kings of England and Marcher lords in the thirteenth century was not a war between the English and the Welsh (even if it came to be construed as such),[19] nor did it involve a denial of the ultimate superiority of the king of England (his right to the homage and fealty of the prince of Gwynedd/Wales was never challenged); rather was it a dispute about the character and contents of the overlordship of the king of England and about the relative range of the superiorities that both of them claimed.

Overlordship was, therefore, precarious. The best that could often be said of an overlord, as it was said of Roger Mortimer in mid-Wales in 1202, was that at that moment he enjoyed supremacy (*cujus dominator tunc erat Rogerus de Mortuomari*).[20] Overlordship, of its very nature, could not be exclusive; it assumed that others participated in the exercise of lordship. A stable state was unlikely to prevail for long in the relationship between overlord and dependant; when circumstances permitted, one of them would strive to increase his share of *dominium*. Thus one of the Welsh vassals of the earl of Gloucester as lord of Glamorgan showed how little he cared for the lord's authority by daring to confirm the earl's own grants;[21] it was but a small step from such temerity to throw off any dependence on the earl, ally with his enemies and even wage open war on him. In such circumstances the earl had but two options – either to see the effective disappearance of his claim to lordship or to assert his authority and intensify his lordship. In common with many of his fellow magnates in Wales and Ireland he chose the latter course.

There is, as might be expected, no single chronology or universal formula to this process of the intensification of lordship. As with conquest itself it depended very much on the initiative of individual lords; the gains made in one generation might be lost in the next, especially during a minority. Thus in both Wales and Ireland the remarkable purposefulness and ambition of William Marshal and his four sons as earls of Pembroke and lords of

[19] As in the preface to the Treaty of Montgomery, 1267: *Litt. Wallie*, p. 1.
[20] T. Jones (ed.), ‘ “Cronica de Wallia” and other documents from Exeter Cathedral Library Ms. 3514’, *Bulletin of the Board of Celtic Studies* 12 (1946–8), 6.
[21] Clark (ed.), *Cartae de Glamorgan*, vol. III, p. 927.

Chepstow and Leinster 1189–1245 transformed the quality, and profitability, of the lordship which they exercised in both countries. In Glamorgan, likewise, two successive earls of Gloucester – Earl Richard (d. 1262) and his son Earl Gilbert 'the Red' (d. 1295) – were above all responsible for converting the lordship from a frontier district into a powerful and profitable Marcher lordship, yielding an income which of itself would be considered a sufficient endowment for an English earl. In Ireland, the same truism is illustrated by the de Burghs, lords of Connacht and, from 1263, earls of Ulster. Earl Walter (d. 1271) and his son Earl Richard 'the Red' (d. 1326) showed triumphantly that in spite of their daunting problems and the enormous range of their lands, they could be highly 'effective provincial lords'; yet within a few years of Earl Richard's death much of their empire lay in ruins.[22]

Over and above the drive and enterprise of individual lords, however, it may be possible to detect certain structural changes of attitudes which might also be said to contribute to the intensification of lordship. Many of the Anglo-Norman lords in Ireland and most of those in Wales also held estates in England and turned in English political and social circles. There they would be familiar – and ever more so as the twelfth and thirteenth centuries advanced – with a pattern of lordship in which there were clear lines of delegation, authority and responsibility and in which services and obligations were closely defined. Such habits of authority and lordship could not, perhaps, be readily transferred to Wales or Ireland; but neither could they be forgotten or ignored. Least of all could they be overlooked in a society in which obligations were increasingly committed to writing. Lordship whose authority was based in writing was of itself a more exacting lordship; it introduced the habits and mentality of literacy into a customary world. Within that world it must have often been regarded as a new-fangled and dangerous practice, part of the *subtilitas modernorum* of the invaders.[23] How much writing was regarded as a potent instrument in the intensification of lordship can be seen time and again in the way in which the restoration of former relationships between the king of England and his client rulers in the British Isles was accompanied by the surrender of *written* instruments. Thus William the Lion in 1189 paid Richard I ten thousand marks in order to secure, among other concessions, the cancellation of the 'new charters' (*novas cartas*) exacted from him by Henry II in 1174; in 1215 the clause of Magna Carta which gave the greatest joy to Llywelyn ab Iorwerth was that (58) which restored to him the charters of submission

---

22 For the earls of Gloucester see in particular, J. B. Smith, 'The Lordships of Glamorgan', *Morgannwg*, 2 (1958), pp. 9–37 and M. Altschul in Pugh (ed.), *Glamorgan County History*, vol. III, ch. 2. For De Burgh power *NHI*, vol. II, pp. 353–5 and R. Frame, *Colonial Ireland*, pp. 31–2.

23 For the phrase *subtilitas modernorum* see M. T. Clanchy, 'The Franchise of Return of Writs', *Transactions Royal Historical Society*, 5th series, 17 (1967), 79.

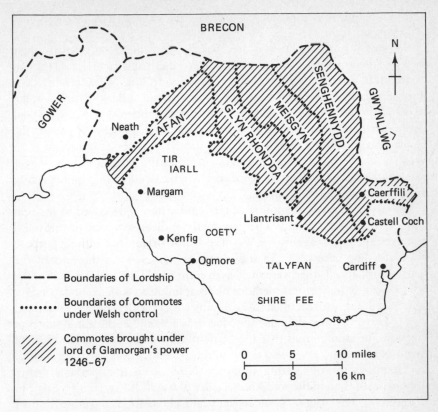

Map 4 The Lordship of Glamorgan in the thirteenth century

extracted from him under compulsion in 1211; in 1237, likewise, part of the comprehensive Anglo-Scottish agreement known as the Treaty of York included the restoration of what were properly regarded as the demeaning writings and documents (*scripta vel instrumenta*) associated with submissions of 1209–12.[24] Written instruments were regularly used to provide the justification for a dramatic intensification of lordship. When Henry III wanted to oust Áed Ó Conchobair from Connacht in order to promote the ambitions of Richard de Burgh he found a ready pretext to hand in the fact that 'by the charter of King John granted to Cathal (Áed's father) he held that land only so long as he should faithfully serve this king'.[25] Not for the last time in the history of colonial power, written legal instruments were used to provide a veneer of legality for crude dispossession; native societies found themselves

---

[24] Stones (ed.), *Anglo-Scottish Relations*, pp. 13, 48–9; J. B. Smith, 'Magna Carta and the Charters of the Welsh Princes', (cited above, ch. 4, n. 37), pp. 344–62.
[25] *CDI*, vol. I, p. 212.

seduced, compromised, confused and undone by novel technologies and procedures.

Nor was it kings alone who used written instruments to intensify their lordship; their magnates followed suit. Thus the earl of Ulster left Áed Ó Néill in no doubt as to the nature of his submission to him or the penalties for disobedience by spelling them out clearly in writing.[26] Likewise in Wales, the Marshals in the south-east and the Mortimers in the middle March served notice of their expansionist ambitions and their anxiety to ensure the permanence of their gains by extorting formal charters of quitclaim from Welsh nobles.[27] Submissions, hostages, promises and tributes were no longer enough; the rule of the written word was to make overlordship more precise, more vertebrate, more enduring.

Military pressure was another of the regular means deployed to reaffirm and intensify overlordship. The apparently endless sequence of raids and punitive expeditions against the Welsh and the Irish were not without purpose nor were they necessarily an indication of weakness on the part of the Anglo-Normans. Rather were they, as in earlier and later empires, one of the acknowledged and regular methods of disciplining a recalcitrant dependant and reminding him of the obligations of subjection. Castles could be, and were, used to perform much the same function. It is not only in the initial stages of invasion and domination that the castle played a key rôle in the story of Anglo-Norman success; it was equally crucial in the secondary stage, that of the intensification of existing authority. Nowhere is this, perhaps, better demonstrated than in the well-known story of Caerffili (Caerphilly) castle in Glamorgan. The Anglo-Normans had laid claim to the overlordship of Glamorgan by the late-eleventh century; but it was to be another hundred and fifty years before they began to convert that claim into direct authority over much of the uplands of the lordship. It was a process which has been aptly termed 'a secondary conquest'. One obvious target for this secondary conquest was the cantref of Senghennydd extending northwards in a narrow strip from Cardiff. Early in 1267 Gilbert de Clare, lord of Glamorgan, showed that he meant business by leading an expedition into Senghennydd, capturing its native lord, Gruffudd ap Rhys, and dispatching him to prison in Kilkenny, one of the Clare castles in Ireland. Earl Gilbert immediately set about building a new castle at Caerffili to demonstrate his newly established authority over the district. During the next five years the earl was engaged in a prolonged struggle for control of the area with Llywelyn ap Gruffudd, prince of Wales; for both the struggle was crucial to their credibility with their followers and to their authority over their dependants. It was Earl Gilbert who emerged triumphant. The castle at Caerffili, 'the greatest baronial stronghold yet built

[26] *H.M.C. De L'Isle and Dudley Mss.*, vol. I, pp. 32–33.
[27] *Calendar of Charter Rolls*, vol. I, p. 198; J. B. Smith, 'The Middle March in the Thirteenth Century', *Bulletin of the Board of Celtic Studies*, 24 (1970–2), 88–93.

in the British Isles', stood as the memorial of his determination and of his victory.²⁸ The splendour of Caerffili castle may, paradoxically, tempt the historian to concentrate too exclusively on its military and architectural significance. Castles, after all, were only a means to an end, the exercise of power and lordship. The massive investment in the castle at Caerffili indicated the determination of the Clares to turn their loose overlordship of upland Glamorgan into direct lordship. Nor did Caerffili stand alone. Castles were likewise built or rebuilt by the Clares at Neath, Kenfig, Llantrisant and Castell Coch for the same purpose.

There was, of course, nothing unique in the methods pursued by the Clares. Other Anglo-Norman lords likewise used the castle as an instrument for intensifying their authority over native dependencies and dynasties. The Marshals were certainly at it in Wales, and doubtless also in Ireland (as at Kilkenny and Carlow). Some of their most magnificent castles – such as Chepstow, Usk and Pembroke – were in securely controlled areas and were massively extended, replanned and refurbished to display to all the wealth and power of the family. But others were built to overawe the Welsh and, literally, to petrify them into a more sustained and exacting submission: such was Cilgerran in south-west Wales, 'an ornate castle of mortar and stones' as the Welsh chronicler said in amazement, built by William Marshal in 1223;²⁹ such also in the south-east were the castles of Caerleon and Machen, both of them commanding territories which the Anglo-Normans had been trying to bring more effectively under their control since the late eleventh century. The de Burghs were faced with very similar problems in Ireland and their response was similar. Their claims to overlordship were massive, but it was only by strenuous effort that such claims could be given some effective content. Richard de Burgh, the 'Red Earl' of Ulster (d. 1326), showed how such effort might be directed. Soon after 1300 he began to build a formidable castle at Northburgh (now Greencastle) in the Inishowen peninsula, reminiscent in many of its features of Edward I's castles in north Wales. Its purpose was clear and identical with that of Caerffili: to show that this area was within the reach of his military power and thereby of his direct lordship. Much at the same time he commissioned the building of a new castle at Ballymote to strengthen the defences of his newly-acquired manor of Sligo.³⁰

Domination, effective domination, required sustained and massive invest-

---

28 Among many accounts the following in particular may be mentioned: J. E. Lloyd, 'Llywelyn ap Gruffydd and the Lordship of Glamorgan', *Archaeologia Cambrensis*, 6th series, 13 (1913), 56–64; F. M. Powicke, *King Henry III and the Lord Edward* (Oxford, 1947), vol. II, pp. 577–82; M. Altschul in Pugh (ed.), *Glamorgan County History*, vol. III, pp. 54–6; J. B. Smith, *Llywelyn ap Gruffudd*, pp. 239–50. The quotations are taken from *Glamorgan County History*, vol. III, pp. 29, 56.

29 *Brut*, p. 100.

30 McNeill, *Anglo-Norman Ulster* (as cited above, ch. 1, n. 29), pp. 73–4; *NHI*, vol. II, p. 220; Otway-Ruthven, *Ireland*, p. 216.

ment; the remains of the castles built in Wales and Ireland in the thirteenth and early-fourteenth centuries bear witness to that fact. Effective domination also required remarkable patience and pertinacity. Outside the lowlands it was rarely secured by a single victory or a simple conquest; instead it had to be won over the generations, as client princelings and chiefs were gradually trounced and cajoled into reliable and submissive dependence. Another example from upland Glamorgan may serve to illustrate the time-scale and the nature of the process.[31] During the twelfth century a native Welsh dynasty exercised hegemony over the commote of Afan and the western uplands of Glamorgan and to some degree over the lowlands west of the river Ogwr (Ogmore). As the Anglo-Normans moved westwards they increasingly impinged on this dynasty's sphere of authority. Temporary accords were no doubt struck between invaders and natives; concessions were made on either side; and accommodations reached. Such arrangements – like those on the borders of most expanding empires – were exceptionally fragile, especially as more and more lowland districts were absorbed into Anglo-Norman hands or used as endowments for the Cistercian monasteries of Margam and Neath. The native dynasty occasionally struck back, ignoring any accords it had made with the new lords of the lowlands. It led, or participated in, periodic raids on Anglo-Norman castles from Neath to Cardiff; it sought to escape the tightening grip of Anglo-Norman lordship by placing itself under the protection of a Welsh potentate, either the prince of Deheubarth or the prince of Gwynedd. For over a century the Anglo-Norman lords of Glamorgan had to be content with the loosest of overlordship, if that, over the native dynasty of Afan. It was only in the thirteenth century that the dynasty began to be drawn into what may be regarded as a regular and civilian relationship of subjection and obedience. By the middle of the century the head of the dynasty was acknowledging the jurisdictional competence of the county court of Cardiff and recognizing the rights of the lord of Glamorgan's bailiffs over his tenants. Domination by judicial process was being substituted for overlordship by raids and parleys. The native dynasty eventually decided that it was easier to swim with the tide than against it. The head of the house, Morgan Gam, had suffered the chastening experience of imprisonment at the hands of the lord of Glamorgan from 1228 to 1230; his successors decided that it was more comfortable to make a graceful submission and to come to terms with the new world of the victors. One of them married the daughter and heir of one of the Anglo-Norman lords of the lowlands; another adopted the Normanized surname 'de Avene' to display to all and sundry its new-founded affiliations. It had taken over a century and a half to absorb the dynasty of Afan and the

---

[31] Smith and Altschul in *Glamorgan County History*, vol. III, chs. 1–2; Altschul, *A Baronial Family in Medieval England*, pp. 56–69; Matthew Griffiths, 'Native Society on the Anglo-Norman Frontier: The Evidence of the Margam Charters', *Welsh History Review*, 14 (1988–9), pp. 179–216.

lands and peoples under its control into the empire of the Anglo-Norman lords of Glamorgan and to teach it to accept the tenurial, jurisdictional, civilian and, even in some respects, the social terms on which that empire was ruled. The tactics that had been employed to achieve that end combined force with persuasion, as the occasion demanded. Similar tactics were deployed throughout Wales and Ireland to bring loosely-attached native satellites into closer and more regular subjection. In the late 1230s, for example, Earl Gilbert Marshal of Pembroke (d. 1241) can be glimpsed trying to tie one of the heirs of the native dynasty of Deheubarth, Maelgwn Fychan (d. 1257), to him tenurially and matrimonially – insisting that he do homage to the earl, hold his lands of him, and marry his son to the earl's daughter.[32] It is an example of the intensification of lordship in action; its ultimate result would be to transform the nature of domination.

An intensified lordship required palpable and regular display of its authority and a closer definition of its rights, particularly in three areas – military service, tenurial relationship and jurisdictional supervision. These were the cardinal spheres within which foreign lordship, be it that of king or aristocracy, was intensified over native society in the thirteenth century. In medieval society the performance of military service was one of the most obvious and minimal obligations of clientship. It was the honourable and acceptable face of dependence. Neither the kings of Scotland nor the princes of Wales and Ireland considered it to be unacceptably demeaning to serve in the king of England's armies; on the contrary, the obligation of joining the host of the over-king was a well accepted feature of power-relationships within native society. Native communities likewise freely accepted the obligation of military service: the men of Iâl (Yale) in north-east Wales, for example, readily recognized that they were bound to serve with their English lord in person and at his pleasure in England, Wales, Scotland and elsewhere for reasonable wages.[33] What was lacking, however, in this recognition of the obligation of military service by client princes and communities was the specific relationship between land tenure and military quotas to which English society was habituated. English kings and lords tried to instil such specificity into the relationship. In 1212 King John inserted a clause into his agreement with two of the claimants to Gwynedd which insisted, for the first time as far as we know, on an annual render and the obligation of military service. Henry III took the issue further in 1247 when he imposed the first known precise military obligation on the rulers of Gwynedd – 1,000 footmen and 24 well-armed horsemen in Wales, a smaller contingent in England.[34] Lords might follow suit: inquisitions taken in the fourteenth century reveal that the Irish chieftains

32 *Litt. Wallie*, pp. 38–9 (the most likely date is 1240–1); *Curia Regis Rolls* (16 vols., London, 1922–78), vol. XVI, pp. 287–90.
33 Davies, *Lordship and Society in the March of Wales*, p. 81.
34 T. D. Hardy (ed.), *Rotuli Chartarum 1199–1216* (London, 1837), p. 188b; *Litt. Wallie*, p. 7.

of Ulster owed the de Burgh earls precise levels of military service.[35] What had been once the honorary duties of clientship was being converted into a precise obligation. Overlordship was being intensified. Contemporaries recognized as much. That is why the Scots objected in 1295 when the king of England demanded military service of their king.[36] Here was one of the thresholds of tolerance of dependence, where a genial overlordship crossed over into being an unacceptable domination.

Land tenure and the control of the descent of land were another such threshold. The acceptance of overlordship did not of necessity require or imply tenurial or territorial dependence. Submission was personal, not territorial. There is no reason to believe, for example, that the Irish princes who submitted to Henry II in 1171–2 in any way regarded themselves as having surrendered their lands to him or as holding their lands henceforth of him. Likewise the Treaty of Windsor in 1175 acknowledged that Ruaidrí Ó Conchobair, king of Connacht, 'holds his land as fully and peacefully as he held it before the lord king entered Ireland'.[37] Domination and overlordship could be effective without interfering with timeless, pre-existent rights over land.

Yet in a society, such as that of Anglo-Norman England, where land was power and where concepts of tenure, of holding land of a superior, were so deeply ingrained it was well nigh inevitable that a claim to overlordship should often be quickly followed by a claim to control over the client's land. Indeed native chieftains occasionally allowed, or even encouraged, such a development for their own purposes. None more so than the powerful Ó Conchobair family of Connacht.[38] Cathal Crobderg Ó Conchobair, king of Connacht 1189–1224, struck a series of accords with King John whose consequence, whether he realized it or not, was to place his lands virtually at the disposal of the king of England. He agreed to surrender a proportion of his lands – as much as two-thirds of them according to one bargain – into the king's hands; he acknowledged an obligation to pay him an annual rent; and in September 1215 he allowed King John to grant him by charter what was his own, 'the whole land of Connacht with all its appurtenances to have and to hold of us and our heirs to him and his heirs, as long as they serve us well'. It was nothing less than the total surrender of ultimate territorial control of Connacht into the hands of the English overlord. Domination had been dramatically intensified without a blow being struck. The reasons for such an outrageous surrender are not far to seek. Cathal had been enticed by the prospect of holding Connacht on clear hereditary terms (*hereditarie*) according to feudal custom; this would

[35] R. Frame, *English Lordship in Ireland 1318–1361* (Oxford, 1982), p. 43.
[36] Barrow, *Bruce*, pp. 62–3.
[37] Roger of Howden, *Chronica*, vol. II, p. 84.
[38] The most recent account will be found in James Lydon, 'Lordship and Crown: Llywelyn of Wales and O'Connor of Connacht', in Davies (ed.), *The British Isles 1100–1500*, pp. 48–63, where full references are given.

have greatly strengthened his hand against the competing claims of the various segments of his own dynasty. He had also been enticed – like many native princes before and after him – by the prospect of the support of the king of England against the greedy ambitions of English barons in Ireland (several of whom had received large speculative grants in Connacht from John from the 1190s onwards). Viewed in those terms Cathal's actions were not as suicidal as they first seem. What he had not bargained for, however, was King John's duplicity: on the very same day in September 1215 that the king gave Cathal and his heirs the title to Connacht by charter, an almost precisely identical grant of Connacht (though one which was doubtless kept secret) was made to Richard de Burgh. Cathal Crobderg had played directly into the king's hands. Furthermore the clause in the 1215 charter making the grant of Connacht to the Ó Conchobair contingent on the fatal phrase 'as long as they shall serve us well' meant that the screw of an intensified lordship could be wound tighter whenever it suited the king.[39] That is precisely what the Ó Conchobair found out to their cost.

The king of England had taken advantage of the anxieties of Cathal Crobderg to bring the kingdom of Connacht into tenurial dependence on his crown. Even without the unwitting connivance of native leaders, it was natural that English kings and lords should wish to construe their lordship over native princes and chieftains in terms with which they were familiar, in other words in terms of the tenurial practice of feudal society. Domination in all periods involves imposing, consciously or otherwise, the terminology and relationships of the world of the dominant partner on his client or dependant. In the feudal world of the Anglo-Normans land was a crucial element in the relationship between lord and vassal; dependence involved the exaction of obligations, annual or occasional, in respect of land so held and the capacity to discipline a recalcitrant vassal through the confiscation of such land. These were the assumptions that now began to be applied to regulate relationships with native rulers in Wales and Ireland.

It is at the level of relationships with the kings of England that the documentation, as usual, allows us to see the process most clearly at work. Two illustrative examples may be chosen, Thomond in Ireland and Gwynedd in Wales. Domnall Mór Ó Briain (d. 1194) of Thomond was one of the Irish princes who had quickly made his peace with Henry II in 1171.[40] He met Henry on the river Suir, submitted to him and agreed to pay a tribute. In other words, he had accepted Henry's overlordship; but he had not compromised the territorial integrity or status of his kingdom. It was during the thirteenth century that the situation changed dramatically. Not only was much of the kingdom of the Ó Briain filched from them; even what was left to them came to be held on clearly dependent tenurial terms – endowment by the king's

---

[39] *Rotuli Chartarum 1199–1216*, pp. 218–19.
[40] See in general Orpen, *Ireland under the Normans*, vol. IV, pp. 53–60.

charter, annual farms, entry fines on succession, and clauses which made tenure contingent on good service.[41] It was the experience of Connacht all over again. It was experience with which the rulers of Gwynedd became all too familiar in the thirteenth century. It was the succession to the principality of Gwynedd after the death of Llywelyn the Great in 1240 which provided the English crown with the opportunity to define and intensify its authority over this most powerful of native Welsh polities.[42] The heir to Gwynedd travelled to Gloucester in that year not only to do homage to the king of England but also 'to receive his territory legally from him'.[43] The clear implication was that he held his land by royal gift. It was an implication which was specifically spelt out in solemn treaties in 1241 and 1247.[44] Thereafter it became the orthodox view in English court circles: as a royal memorandum put it in 1276, 'the ancestors of Llywelyn ap Gruffudd always held their lands of Wales of the kings of England'.[45] Overlordship had hardened in the English official mind into tenurial dependence; it was by such sleights of memory that dominion was intensified. Once tenurial dependence was assumed, claimed or acknowledged the position of the native leader – the prince of Gwynedd or king of Connacht or of Thomond – could be more closely approximated to that of an English magnate. Edward I made the point eloquently when he referred to Llywelyn ap Gruffudd in 1276 as 'one of the greater among the other magnates of our kingdom'.[46]

Kings intensified their tenurial control; so did lords, though the documentation for their activities is sparse and often late in date. In 1331, for example, Domnall Ó Hanlon, king of Oirthir, surrendered all his rights and lands to William de Burgh, earl of Ulster, and agreed to hold them henceforth as a tenant of the earl and on specific conditions.[47] Such a tenurial link frequently afforded the lord an opportunity to insert clauses which spelt out menacingly the precariousness of the tenant's position and thereby made him more deeply beholden to his lord. In 1241 and again in 1247 Henry III inserted clauses in his agreements with the prince of Gwynedd stipulating that any breach of the agreements would lead to the confiscation of the lands of the princes in perpetuity and also, in 1241, making the king the prince's heir should the latter die without a legitimate heir of his body.[48] A similar clause was added to the terms offered to Conchobar Ó Briain of Thomond in 1250 and security was taken from him that he would not alienate his land; while in an agreement

[41] Among the key documents are those in *CDI*, vol. I, pp. 160–1, 455, 464.
[42] See in general Lloyd, *History of Wales*, vol. II, ch. 19; Davies, *Conquest*, pp. 300–7; Smith, *Llywelyn ap Gruffudd*, pp. 27–66.
[43] *Brut (RBH.)*, pp. 236–7; Luard (ed.), *Annales Monastici*, vol. I, p. 115.
[44] *Litt. Wallie*, pp. 7, 9.
[45] *Anc. Corr. conc. Wales*, p. 252.
[46] P. Chaplais (ed.), *Treaty Rolls 1234–1325* (London, 1955), p. 54 ('qui est unus de maioribus inter magnates alios regni nostri').
[47] Katherine Simms in *Seanchas Ard Mhacha*, 9 (1978–9), 89–90.
[48] *Litt. Wallie*, pp. 11, 8.

made between the earl of Kildare and Donnchadh Ó Ceallaigh a century later the earl was specifically permitted to re-seize the land in the event of failure to perform services.[49] What we are witnessing in these and many similar instances is a deliberate attempt to bring native society, at the level of leaders and communities alike, more firmly within the authority of lordship and within the ambit of its rules. The *dominus superior* was being converted into a *dominus terrae*. It is a familiar episode of the intensification of the powers of domination in different parts of the world in many different periods.[50]

The other obvious route to the intensification of authority was through the assertion of judicial superiority. Justice and lordship were intimately associated in the medieval mind; to accept a lord's authority was to acknowledge the obligation to attend his court and, thereby, to recognize his jurisdiction. It was inevitable, therefore, that even the loosest overlordship should occasionally bare its jurisdictional teeth. Already in 1093, according to the Worcester chronicler, William Rufus had tried to insist that Malcolm III of Scotland should be judicially answerable in the king of England's court (*in curia sua rectitudinem ei faceret*). Malcolm retorted that Scottish kings were only accustomed to answer judicially to the kings of the English on the borders of their kingdom and that on such occasions judgement was given by the magnates of both kingdoms, not by the barons of the king of England alone.[51] The altercation makes it clear that contemporaries recognized how politically menacing claims to jurisdictional superiority indeed were. The Welsh princelings were not in such a strong position to resist the jurisdictional advances of the English as was the Scottish monarchy. In 1104 the leading prince of Powys was summoned before the king's council at Shrewsbury, tried in a day-long trial, and found guilty and imprisoned, 'not' (as the Welsh annalist loudly protests) 'by law, but through might and power and violation of the law'.[52] Not for the first or last time a more exacting overlordship was securing its aims beneath a claim to jurisdictional superiority and a veneer of judicial procedure.

Claims to jurisdictional superiority surface occasionally in the twelfth century but it is in the thirteenth century that they come to occupy centre stage in the definition of relationships between suzerain and client in the British Isles. The remarkable growth of English royal documentation in the decades immediately after 1200 may indeed make the contrast appear sharper than in reality it was; but that an important shift in emphasis took place hardly admits of doubt. The central explanation for that shift lies in momentous changes in attitudes towards law and jurisdiction throughout Europe from the mid-twelfth century onwards.[53] Customary laws were systematized and codified;

---

49 *CDI*, vol. I, p. 455; *Red Book of Kildare*, p. 154.
50 See, for example, the description of a similar process of individualizing the tenure of land in New Zealand from the 1860s in P. Mason, *Patterns of Dominance* (as in ch. 1, n. 47) p. 116.
51 Florence of Worcester, *Chronicon*, vol. II, p. 31.   52 *Brut*, p. 26.
53 See in general Susan Reynolds, *Kingdoms and Communities in Western Europe 900–1300* (Oxford, 1984), ch. 2.

the legislative and judicial powers of kings and princes began to be more clearly proclaimed; the boundaries and hierarchies of competing and contiguous jurisdictions were more closely defined; a legal profession began to emerge and with it new legal norms and concepts. In particular, with respect to the present argument, notions of jurisdiction in error and of appeals to a sovereign jurisdictional source, first made familiar through eccesiastical practice, became common; while relative political power and suzerainty were increasingly expressed in legal and jurisdictional terms, notably in the assumption of the ultimate judicial answerability of all subordinate jurisdictions. It was notions such as these that now began to be applied to define, and thereby to intensify, the relationships between overlords (especially the king of England) and native rulers within the British Isles. The results were momentous, first in Wales and later in Scotland.

Already in 1201, in the first surviving formal agreement between a king of England and a Welsh prince, King John had given an indication of things to come. The agreement was in effect a treaty (*forma pacis*) between an overlord and a client prince; but it broached at some length, albeit cautiously, the question of the judicial supervision that the overlord might exercise in land pleas involving the client prince. John may have tiptoed cautiously around the issue of jurisdiction *vis à vis* Gwynedd in 1201; he showed no such restraint in his attitude towards the prince of Powys in 1208, reminding him forcefully that 'he would be judicially answerable in the court of the king at the royal summons'.[54] This judicial masterfulness was displayed towards other Welsh princelings during the thirteenth century as and when the opportunity arose: thus in the 1240s the princelings of Deheubarth were forced to acknowledge that they were obliged to appear in the king's court at Carmarthen, while the prince of Gwynedd was likewise required 'to stand to justice in the court of my lord the king', notably in cases relating to the inheritance and division of his principality.[55] It was Edward I, with characteristic thoroughness, who took the argument of the suzerain's jurisdictional superiority to its logical conclusion. He selected evidence from the plea rolls, and set up a commission, to prove that 'the king's ancestors were wont to rule and adjudge a prince of Wales and a Welsh baron of Wales and their peers and others their inferiors and peers'.[56] He made it abundantly clear to Llywelyn ap Gruffudd that he was ultimately obliged 'to do and receive right in the court of the kings of England', to proceed by their writs and to appear before their justices; he even hinted that commissioners might be sent into Gwynedd itself to review decisions given in the prince's courts.[57] This was a calculated intensification of

[54] Rymer (ed.), *Foedera*, vol. i, part i, pp. 84, 101.
[55] *Close Rolls 1237–42*, pp. 348–9; *1247–51*, p. 113; *Litt. Wallie*, p. 9; *Calendar of Patent Rolls 1247–58*, pp. 362, 432.
[56] *Calendar of Various Chancery Rolls 1277–1326* (London, 1912), pp. 188, 190.
[57] *Anc. Corr. conc. Wales*, p. 252; Davies (ed.), *Welsh Assize Roll*, pp. 59–60; *Cal. Various Chancery Rolls 1277–1326*, pp. 173–5, 211.

lordship; it involved nothing less than the belittlement of the vassal. It was a Scottish chronicler who best registered amazement at what was happening. 'The Welsh', he remarked, 'who are the descendants of the Britons . . . are now compelled to go to London to have their suits determined by the judgement of the English.'[58]

But the tactics of judicial intensification could be directed at the Scots likewise. It is true that, with the exception of the years 1174–89, the kings of Scotland (unlike the princelings of Wales) had probably never specifically acknowledged any feudal dependence on the kings of England in respect of their kingdom. To that extent the formal legal pretext for intensifying the king of England's claim to overlordship over Scotland was lacking. Even Edward I was to concede in 1290 that the Scottish kingdom was, and was to remain, 'separate, free in itself and without subjection to the English kingdom'.[59] Nevertheless, the king of England found it difficult to resist the temptation to assume an attitude of judicial superiority towards the king of Scotland on occasion. King John showed such judicial highhandedness in Magna Carta (clause 59) when he determined that the claims of the young Alexander II should be dealt with by the same rules as were applied 'to our other barons of England' and that 'by judgement of peers in the king's court'. Any claims to jurisdictional intervention lay dormant throughout the thirteenth century; but they erupted with explosive force in November 1292. Within one week of the accession of John Balliol as king of Scotland (17 November 1292), a burgess of Berwick submitted to Edward I a series of petitions against judgements given in the court of the Guardians, the highest court in Scotland, during the interregnum after Alexander III's death in 1286. It was a deliberate test case. To the dismay of the Scots, Edward accepted that he would hear whatever appeals might be brought and, if necessary, summon the king of Scotland himself to appear.[60] It was a shattering demonstration of what was meant by the intensification of judicial lordship, all the more shattering since there was no precedent for it and indeed firm promises to the contrary.

What happened in Wales gradually and in Scotland dramatically may not have been consciously planned; but its end result was clear and clearly willed. The king of England was intensifying his authority over men whom he regarded as client rulers to the point that he was transforming both the nature of their power within their own polities and his relationship with them. His claim to ultimate judicial superiority compromised the integrity of their dominions (much as his own authority in Gascony was undermined by the right of appeal to the parlement of Paris); it also gave him the opportunity to

---

[58] Anderson, *Early Sources of Scottish History*, vol. II, p. 527.
[59] J. Stevenson (ed.), *Documents Illustrative of the History of Scotland 1286–1306* (2 vols., Edinburgh, 1870), vol. I, p. 167.
[60] Stevenson (ed.), *Documents on the History of Scotland*, vol. I, pp. 376–89; Barrow, *Bruce*, pp. 51–3; Michael Prestwich, *Edward I* (London, 1988), pp. 370–1.

dabble in the internal politics of Wales and Scotland and thereby, if need be, to destabilize them. Native rulers recognized that the end result of such policies was to undermine their authority and credibility; as Llywelyn ap Gruffudd put it, it was 'the disgrace to ourselves' that was truly pernicious.[61] He was right. The next stage would be to summon the client rulers to the English parliament, thereby putting them on a par with the magnates of the realm of England. Edward I seems to have had such a proposal in mind for both Llywelyn ap Gruffudd of Wales and John Balliol of Scotland. At such a parliament petitions from Wales and Scotland would be considered alongside those from England, Ireland and Gascony by the king of England and his councillors. That is indeed what happened in the Lenten parliament of 1305. The end result of the process of judicial intensification was apparent for all to see.[62]

There were other ways in which the king of England could drive home his superiority over those whom he regarded as subordinate, client rulers. He could show his ultimate political supremacy, as Henry III did *vis à vis* the ruler of Gwynedd in the 1240s, by requiring them to receive and execute the king's commands or to promise not to receive outlaws from the lands of the king or his barons. He might command them not to build castles or establish markets in their territories without the king's permission.[63] Most insidiously, the client ruler's control over his own major subjects – and thereby the political stability of his regime – could be severely compromised by an insistence that those subjects owed an overriding allegiance to the king of England as their overlord. Henry II had used this device to abase William the Lion of Scotland after his capture in 1174: he required all the leading Scottish ecclesiastics to swear fealty to him 'as liege lord' and the lay barons to do homage to him and his heirs against all men.[64] Similar tactics were regularly used to cut the princes of Gwynedd down to size in the thirteenth century: in 1211 King John showed the completeness of his triumph over Llywelyn ab Iorwerth by reserving to the English crown the allegiance of such of Llywelyn's men as the king should choose: in the 1240s Gwynedd's claim to the leadership of native Wales was completely punctured by the king's insistence that 'the homage and services of all the barons and nobles of Wales' were reserved exclusively to the king; in 1277, after his crushing victory over Llywelyn ap Gruffudd, Edward I with characteristic ruthlessness took the campaign of political belittlement deep into Gwynedd itself, by requiring twenty men from each *cantref* of Llywelyn's principality to swear annually that they would withdraw from the prince's fealty, homage, lordship and service if the prince failed to observe the terms of the treaty recently imposed on him.[65] Edward I was given a similar oppor-

---

[61] *Anc. Corr. conc. Wales*, p. 91.   [62] See below, pp. 124, 127.
[63] *Litt. Wallie*, pp. 9–12; *Anc. Corr. conc. Wales*, p. 86.
[64] Stones (ed.), *Anglo-Scottish Relations*, pp. 2–5.
[65] J. B. Smith, 'Magna Carta and the Charters of the Welsh Princes', 362; *Litt. Wallie*, pp. 6, 8–9, 121.

tunity to intensify his power, albeit in very different circumstances, in Scotland in the early 1290s; he seized it ruthlessly with both hands. In June–July 1291 he secured individual oaths of fealty to himself as 'superior and direct lord of the kingdom of Scotland' from the Guardians of the kingdoms and its leading lords, gentry, freeholders and burgesses.[66]

By whatever route or routes the power of the overlord – be he king or aristocrat – was intensified, the question was likely to arise, sooner or later, whether there was a threshold of tolerance beyond which it could not proceed without provoking the client ruler into revolt. If overlordship became too demanding, did it transform itself into direct lordship? In that case was the relationship between overlord and client ruler so transformed that it had to be redefined, be it by compromise or conquest? In Wales, the history of the native dynasties of Afan (Glamorgan) or of southern Powys (Powys Wenwynwyn) in the thirteenth century shows how native dynasties could come to terms with a more demanding English lordship (seignorial in the one, royal in the other), adjust their pretensions and attitudes to the realities of power, exult (as did the lord of southern Powys) in their new status as 'a baron of the lord king' – and survive.[67] Just as in the response to the original Anglo-Norman penetration, so in the response to the intensification of lordship, compliance and adjustment were certainly one reaction.

But as native rulers and communities came to recognize that the intensification of overlordship involved an unacceptable erosion of their own status and authority, their response could be very different. It might take the form of resistance and revolt. It might also take the form of almost desperate attempts to build theoretical bulwarks against the pretensions of the overlord. It was in that spirit that Llywelyn the Great claimed in 1224 that he had 'no less liberty than the king of Scotland', or that his grandson harped on his status and liberties as a prince. 'The rights of our principality', wrote Llywelyn ap Gruffudd in a famous letter to Edward I in 1273, 'are entirely separate from the rights of your kingdom, although we hold our principality under your royal power'.[68] It is a classic statement of a client prince's view of his rights *vis à vis* his overlord. It was not a view to which the king of England could subscribe. Nor was it a view that prevailed; within ten years the principality of Wales had been finally conquered. A few years later the legal argument was put forward that 'though the land of Scotland is called a realm, it is in fact no more than a lordship or an honour, like Wales or the earldom of Chester or the bishopric of Durham'.[69] Edward I may not have subscribed to such a view; but he soon

66 E. L. G. Stones and G. G. Simpson, *Edward I and the Throne of Scotland 1290–1296* (2 vols., Oxford, 1978), vol. II, pp. 366–70; Barrow, *Bruce*, pp. 37–8.
67 See above p. 98; D. Stephenson, 'The Politics of Powys Wenwynwyn in the Thirteenth Century', *Cambridge Medieval Celtic Studies*, 7 (1984), pp. 39–61; R. Morgan, 'The Barony of Powys 1275–1360', *Welsh History Review*, 10 (1980–1), pp. 1–42.
68 *Anc. Corr. conc. Wales*, pp. 24, 86.
69 Stones and Simpson, *Edward I and the Throne of Scotland*, vol. II, pp. 328–9.

treated Scotland as if it were less than an independent kingdom and demoted it in official terminology to the status of a land, *terra*. By 1300 the principality of Wales and the kingdom of Scotland were, in the eyes of the king of England, no more. That, it might be said, was the end result of the intensification of overlordship.

The intensification of lordship and overlordship was not necessarily a deliberate policy nor was it necessarily consciously pursued with the object of reducing clients and dependants to surrender or revolt. Much depended on accidents and opportunities – on a timely minority, an unexpected death or a disputed succession (as in Wales in 1240 or Scotland in 1290), or on the need to respond to the ill-timed challenge of a client ruler or neighbour (as in Scotland in 1174 and in Wales in 1211 or 1276). Much depended also on the general preoccupations and ambitions of English kings and lords, be they, for example, the Clare or Marshall families or Henry III or Edward I. Yet the intensification of lordship was more than the sum of its individual parts and of fortuitous opportunities. It drew also on changes in the structure of governance and authority, on a growing demand for clear lines of supervision and answerability, on shifts in attitudes towards the nature and expression of dependence, on changed perceptions of the nature of lordship and power. Structures and attitudes have their own momentum; men's actions and responses are shaped by them more profoundly than they think. Changes in assumptions and attitudes in the thirteenth century are the subject of the next chapter; they are also the essential backcloth of the intensification of control discussed in this chapter. Once the process of the intensification of over-lordship had gathered momentum, and especially when it was conducted with the power and determination at the command of the English monarchy, it was a process which almost inevitably led, sooner or later, to confrontation and, thence, either to surrender or conquest.

6

Conquest

'By the death of Christ', so Henry I is alleged to have sworn on one occasion, 'through our great power we commit wrongs and violence against these people [the Welsh]; yet everybody knows that they have a hereditary right to their lands'.[1] Henry I does not perhaps spring most readily to mind as a king given to flaunting a tender conscience or expressing self-doubt about his actions; to that extent we may dismiss the story as apocryphal. But one of Henry's successors, Edward I, likewise felt the need to justify his actions *vis à vis* the Welsh. Wales, he remarked, had come into his possession not only by virtue of his strength but also by way of justice.[2] When kings feel moved to defend themselves, then we may rest assured that others also had twinges of conscience about what was happening in Wales and Ireland. Gerald of Wales is there to bear us out. Gerald was normally too busy cultivating his own ego or defending and extolling his own kinsmen to allow such doubts to worry him; but occasionally his ecclesiastical scruples got the better of him. When he defended Strongbow and Robert fitz Stephen against the charge of being 'mere robbers' he was presumably responding to contemporary criticism of the Anglo-Norman invasion of Ireland. Indeed he himself was driven on one occasion to refer to the 'new and bloodstained acquisition of land, secured at the cost of great bloodshed and the slaughter of a Christian people'.[3] That, of course, was the charge that touched the ecclesiastic on an exposed nerve: conquest and slaughter of pagans might be acceptable, indeed praiseworthy; the conquest of a Christian people was altogether a different matter.

Gerald used all his casuistry to get round the issue; he produced five reasons, and a whole chapter, to explain the title of the English kings to Ireland.[4] A man who needs five reasons to justify his actions is clearly arguing from a weak

[1] *Itin. Kambrie*, p. 35.
[2] *Calendar of Charter Rolls*, vol. II, p. 284, printed in full in *Archaeologia Cambrensis*, 5th ser. vol. 10 (1893), 233–4 ('non tantum virtute potencie set via justicie').
[3] *Expugnatio*, pp. 228–9 (Bk 2. ch. 33), 156–7 (Bk 2. ch. 9).
[4] *Expugnatio*, pp. 148–9 (Bk 2. ch. 6). For some other contemporary arguments explaining how control of Ireland had 'devolved' to the king of England see W. Ullmann, 'On the influence of Geoffrey of Monmouth in English History', in C. Bauer *et al.* (eds.), *Speculum Historiale* (Munich, 1965), pp. 257–76.

position; but Gerald's arguments do in fact broadly reflect the theoretical pretexts that were recurrently rehearsed to justify Anglo-Norman and English domination in Wales, Ireland and Scotland. Some were historical or pseudo-historical. Gerald himself made much use of such arguments to defend the English intervention in Ireland, even though that involved him in pillaging fantasies from Geoffrey of Monmouth (for whom he elsewhere showed contempt) and relying on books of Irish prophecy.[5] None was to follow this line of argument more relentlessly than Edward I who ransacked mythology, chronicles and archives in order to establish his claim to the superior lordship of Scotland.[6] For those who were less than impressed by the appeal to history, there were alternative arguments to hand to justify conquest. Breach of the bond of feudal subjection was one of the most legalistically satisfying. It was on this ground that Edward I justified his actions in both Wales and Scotland.[7] For those who subscribed to his premises there was a neat, self-fulfilling logic about his arguments. Ireland was, of course, much more awkward in this respect, since there was no pre-existing feudal bond between its rulers and the kings of England to justify the original Anglo-Norman invasion. Apologists were, therefore, driven to explain the invasion in terms of Diarmait Mac Murchada's invitation to the Anglo-Normans to come to his aid and, thereafter, of the hereditary right transmitted through Mac Murchada's daughter to her husband, Richard fitz Gilbert, Strongbow. But such an argument, as Gerald of Wales acknowledged, could only take one so far; it might serve to countenance the domination of Leinster but not that of the rest of Ireland. That is where the argument from free-will submission was most useful: it served to justify Henry II's claim to be lord of Ireland, since the Irish kings had submitted willingly to him. Even Edward I, who had not a moment's doubt about the propriety of his actions in Wales and Scotland, felt that his title in both countries could be put beyond any cavil by referring to the total and unconditional surrender of the peoples of both countries.

Such an array of arguments must surely have got most consciences off the hook; but ecclesiastics were still haunted by a niggling doubt about the propriety of conquering a Christian people. Two further arguments were, therefore, trundled out to put their consciences at rest. One was to proclaim that conquest was the due and proper punishment for sin, as the Old Testament only too amply demonstrated. As it happens, this argument coincided with a deep conviction among the native peoples themselves – certainly among the Welsh – that foreign oppression was indeed the divine penalty for their own sinfulness.[9] But the more immediate and convincing

---

[5] *Expugnatio*, pp. 96–7 (Bk 1 ch. 33), 232–3 (Bk 2. ch. 34).
[6] Stones and Simpson, *Edward I and the Throne of Scotland*, vol. I, pp. 137–62.
[7] Statute of Wales 1284, preamble; Stones (ed.), *Anglo-Scottish Relations*, pp. 211–15.
[8] *Expugnatio*, pp. 228–31 (Bk 2. ch. 33); 148–9 (Bk 2. ch. 6).
[9] *Expugnatio*, pp. 232–3 (Bk 2. ch. 34); Davies, *Conquest*, p. 78; *Annals of Loch Cé*, p. 315.

argument lay in the justificatory mechanisms of ecclesiastical procedure. Nowhere was this more so than in Ireland, where other arguments for conquest were patently thin. Adrian IV's bull *Laudabiliter* (1155), supplemented by subsequent letters by Pope Alexander III, made good the deficiencies of those arguments by conferring on the king of England the right to take control of Ireland and to do so for the loftiest of reasons, 'in order to enlarge the boundaries of the Church'.[10] *Laudabiliter* worked wonders for the consciences of contemporary Anglo-Norman ecclesiastics worried about the propriety of conquest. There was no comparable bull to ease their consciences in Wales; but there the feudal arguments were more clear-cut and in any case a well-targeted barrage of excommunications provided an ample smokescreen behind which the English king and aristocracy could get down to the work of conquest without undue scruple.

Conquest was certainly what they were about; nor were they or their successors in any way inhibited about calling it such.[11] Indeed they might have been encouraged to cut through the tedious apologetics and to call a conquest a conquest by the revival of Roman law notions of conquest-right in the twelfth century.[12] Yet for men who were so self-assured about what they were doing and so adept at devising justifications for themselves, what is surely surprising is how slow or reluctant they were to effect what we might call a thorough-going conquest. Indeed the kings of England seem to have kept at arm's length from such a prospect. Such reluctance is not difficult to explain. Until the early thirteenth century the kings of England and many of their magnates had preoccupations and prospects in abundance in England, France and elsewhere without turning their attentions to the outlying and not hugely rewarding parts of the British Isles. As for the concept of a 'final' conquest, the military and governmental challenges it posed were truly daunting and hardly worth the effort when so much could be gained by overlordship and the collection of tribute. Even Gerald of Wales had to admit that the conquest of the whole of Ireland was, at least initially, out of the question;[13] while the vast deployment of men, resources and money that Edward I had to commandeer to effect and sustain the conquest of the remaining areas of north and west Wales was a salutary warning to those who thought that such an enterprise could be undertaken lightly. Administratively, likewise, any attempt to extend an English-based governance to the outlying parts of the British Isles would encounter problems of communication, accountability, personnel, local power-structures, and profound differences in legal traditions and social customs which would call in doubt the wisdom or indeed the feasibility of such an exercise. A full-blooded conquest was scarcely possible because neither the

[10] Curtis and McDowell (eds.), *Irish Historical Documents 1172–1922*, p. 17.
[11] See above, p. 47.
[12] D. W. Sutherland, 'Conquest and Law', *Studia Gratiana*, 15 (1972), pp. 35–51.
[13] *Expugnatio*, pp. 248–9 (Bk 2. ch. 38).

military power to effect it nor the administrative means to sustain it were to hand.

Nevertheless some men came to contemplate the thought of 'a full and complete conquest' (as Gerald of Wales called it). Some may have toyed with such ideas from an early stage: according to Gerald, who was at his most rhetorically inventive in such passages, Robert fitz Stephen dangled before his troops at a critical stage in the Anglo-Norman invasion of Ireland the prospect that 'lordship of the whole kingdom will devolve upon our race in the future'.[14] Yet on the whole early invaders lived from day to day, seizing each opportunity as it came and working to no great master plan. It was only later that the tempo of their activity and the scale of their ambitions changed and that visions of a comprehensive conquest and the sustained imposition of intensive foreign rule began to be regularly entertained, at least by some people. A not dissimilar shift in attitudes has been identified in other frontierlands of conquest and colonization in medieval Europe, such as Spain and the German-Slav frontier, at a certain point in their development; there, likewise, it was accompanied by, and expressed in, a much sharper confront-ational relationship between invading conqueror and native society.[15] In the British Isles a similar change in attitude and emphasis towards client peoples and principalities seems to take place broadly speaking between the reigns of Henry II and Edward I. As with all deep-seated, long-term historical changes, it is easier to feel such a shift in one's historical bones than to document it with chronological precision in a panoply of footnotes. It is the nature and causes of that shift in attitude which will be explored in this final chapter.

Several reasons suggest themselves to explain the shift in attitude. In Wales, Ireland and Scotland profound changes in the structure of political power and ambitions were taking place in the thirteenth century which, potentially at least, had serious implications for relationships with the Anglo-Normans, not least with the king of England himself. In Wales the attempts of the princes of Gwynedd to build a united principality of native Wales and to provide it with institutional and ideological foundations met with a considerable measure of success. Such attempts were leading to a major change in the balance of power in Wales and thereby, ultimately, in relationships with the English aristocracy in Wales and with the king of England.[16] The pattern was different in Ireland; but there likewise the Anglo-Norman momentum was visibly faltering by the mid-thirteenth century. Brian Ó Néill (d. 1260) was putting in a bid to be

---

[14] *Expugnatio*, pp. 230–1 (Bk 2. ch. 34); 48–9 (Bk 1. ch. 9). Cf. the Kilkenny chronicler's reference to 'the full conquest of Scotland', *NHI*, vol. II, p. 274.

[15] R. A. Fletcher, 'Reconquest and Crusade in Spain, *c.* 1050–1150', *Transactions Royal Historical Society*, 5th ser. (1987), 37–8; E. Christiansen, *The Northern Crusades* (London, 1980), p. 250.

[16] R. R. Davies, 'Law and National Identity in Thirteenth Century Wales', in R. R. Davies, *et al.* (eds.), *Welsh Society and Nationhood. Essays to Glanmor Williams* (Cardiff, 1984), pp. 51–69.

regarded as 'king of the Gaels of Ireland'; and 'a new militarily more efficient style of Gaelic opposition' was emerging.[17] As for Scotland, it enjoyed for the most part a remarkable period of cordial relationships with the English monarchy during the thirteenth century; but the growing maturity of its European-type monarchy and the country's increasing awareness of its own 'regnal solidarity' meant that it was now 'one of the recognized powers of middle rank within the family of west European states' and could never willingly revert to the submissive client relationship which it had periodically accepted in the past *vis à vis* the king of England.[18]

But the shift in approach is surely also to be explained by profound changes within political society and governmental attitudes in England itself. They can only be hinted at cursorily here. As lawyers got to work on the terminology of feudal relationships and to spell out more precisely what such obligations might entail; English overlordship became more demanding and aggressive. With the loss of the monarchy's northern French lands in 1204 and the acceptance of that loss in 1259, the English king became more or less permanently resident in England and more likely, therefore, to give closer attention to his overlordship, presumed or otherwise, of the British Isles. As a Westminster-based English governmental machine became increasingly complex and bureaucratic, the possibility of extending its reach beyond the boundaries of England and of introducing its norms in legal habits, administrative structure and financial accountability into other parts of the British Isles on a systematic basis began to be entertained and, indeed, acted upon.

Once these interrelated changes began to gather momentum, there was likely to be, sooner or later, a profound change in the practice and perception of domination. It is with changes in perception that I am particularly concerned, for how men see the world – how it is and how it should be – very considerably shapes how they act and their reasons for doing so. One area in which perceptions changed, or at least were redirected, was with regard to the civilizing mission of the conquerors. Claims to be the agents of civilization were, of course, not new. Conquest and civilization have been close bedfellows throughout history; in the medieval period the Church did much to bless and promote the union. Nowhere more so than in Ireland. The Papacy had provided a whole host of ecclesiastical justifications beforehand to warrant the king of England's invasion – 'to correct evil customs and to plant virtues', 'to make its people obedient to the laws', 'to imbue that nation with good morals' and so forth. As Gerald of Wales put it succinctly, accepting a new political mastery and 'a better pattern of life' (*vivendi forma melior*) went

---

[17] *NHI*, vol. II, p. 244; K. W. Nicholls, 'Anglo-French Ireland and After', *Peritia*, 1 (1982), 372. Cf. the comment in *Annals of Connacht*, p. 93 (1247): 'The Galls of Connacht had not experienced for many a long year the like of the war which these princes now waged against them'.

[18] Reynolds, *Kingdoms and Communities*, p. 261; Barrow, *Kingship and Unity*, p. 155.

naturally hand in hand.[19] Nor were ecclesiastics alone in their zeal to introduce the values of civilized European society to the outer reaches of Britain. David I of Scotland, so William of Malmesbury tells us, was so anxious to do just that in his kingdom that he promised to exempt his barons and knights from the triennial tax if they agreed to adopt a civilized way of life – dressing with more taste and being more particular about their food.[20] King David promoted civilization through bribery and by introducing into the country Norman knights and ecclesiastics who might groom his subjects in the ways of civilized society. Elsewhere in the dark corners of the British Isles civilization was introduced at the point of the sword. As one chronicler put it with disarming frankness, the Anglo-Normans 'perseveringly civilized Wales *after* they had vigorously subdued its inhabitants'.[21] The causal connection between conquest and civilization could not be more succinctly put.

For laymen, as opposed to ecclesiastics, conquest was recurrently justified by reference to two issues in particular – the imposition of peace and good order and the establishment of sound laws. Thus in Wales the Normans prided themselves on having 'encouraged peace and established laws and statutes'; in Ireland Henry II was entrusted with a mission 'to make its people obedient to laws' and was remembered as the man who 'reduced the land and its inhabitants to obedience'.[22] In Scotland Edward I gave a sinister hint of his future intentions in August 1290 when he appointed Anthony Bek, bishop of Durham, as lieutenant there to keep Scotland in tranquillity and – in an ominous phrase, so often used in our own day to justify foreign intervention – 'to reform the state of the country'.[23] No one celebrated the law-and-order mission of the English kings more triumphantly than did the Lanercost chronicler in his comment on Edward I's achievements in Scotland:

Scotia, distraught by lawlessness too long,
Is now, by English Edward's guidance, strong;
... Let Scotia prosper while, from o'er the border,
King Edward shields the cause of law and order.[24]

The Anglo-Normans saw themselves, therefore, from an early date as purveyors of good governance and sound laws to the backward people of the British Isles.

The novelty of their mission in the thirteenth century is that it acquired a much sharper and more intolerant aspect. It was not law and order in general

[19] *Expugnatio*, pp. 145–7 (Bk 2. ch. 5), 100–1 (Bk 1. ch. 35); Curtis and McDowell, *Irish Historical Documents 1172–1922*, pp. 19–22.
[20] William of Malmesbury, *De Gestis Regum*, vol. II, pp. 476–7.
[21] Davis and Potter (eds.), *Gesta Stephani* (as cited above, ch. 1, n. 65), p. 9.
[22] *Gesta Stephani*, pp. 14–15; *Expugnatio*, pp. 144–5 (Bk 2. ch. 5); *Calendar of Papal Registers: Papal Letters* (15 vols. London and Dublin, 1893–1978), vol. I, p. 513.
[23] Rymer, *Foedera*, vol. I, part 2, p. 737; Barrow, *Kingship and Unity*, 159; Prestwich, *Edward I*, p. 362.
[24] H. Maxwell (ed.), *Chronicle of Lanercost 1272–1346* (Glasgow, 1913), pp. 85–6.

that they now purveyed, but *English* law and *English* governmental order in particular. The native laws of Wales and, to a much lesser extent, Ireland had hitherto been grudgingly respected and their separate status acknowledged; now they were scrutinized to discover whether they were 'just and reasonable' or 'displeasing to God and to reason'.[25] At best they were amended and corrected, as were the laws of Wales in 1284 and of Scotland in 1305; at worst they might be condemned outright as 'detestable to God and so contrary to all law that they ought not to be deemed laws', as happened to Irish law in 1277.[26] In terms of governance likewise, the institutions of English administration were now increasingly regarded as the norm. They were exported piecemeal to Ireland from the late twelfth century onwards; they were gradually introduced into districts under royal control in Wales in the thirteenth century and formally imposed as the structure of government for the royal lands there in 1284; and though royal government in Scotland was too sophisticated and too imitative of English practices in many respects to require a major transplant of English institutions, the exchequer established at Berwick in 1297 was specifically to be modelled on the Westminster one.[27] In other words an earlier plurality of custom and approach was increasingly being replaced by an assumption of the superiority and indeed 'naturalness' of *English* law and governance. It is one of the indications that a substantial shift in approach was taking, or had taken, place.

Another indication of that shift of attitudes is the growing categorization of natives and settlers in both Wales and Ireland and the acceptance of that categorization as a basic fact of governance. Categorization was not of itself discriminatory; on the contrary it was an honest acknowledgement that different peoples subject to a common lord or king had different customs, laws, languages, social organization, inheritance practices and so forth. The Anglo-Norman conquerors of Wales and Ireland accepted this plurality from earliest days, as is manifest in the multiple greeting clauses of their writs and in their ready acknowledgement of the differences in laws, modes of punishment, inheritance practices and land renders between native and settler.[28] Such a recognition need not have led to alienation or discrimination; on the contrary, it could well be the basis on which mutual respect could have been founded and gradual assimilation effected. Scotland is there to prove as much. Its ethnic, linguistic, cultural and other divisions were arguably quite as profound as those of Wales and Ireland; yet, during the thirteenth century in particular, a

[25] Davies, *Welsh Assize Roll*, p. 59; Stones (ed.), *Anglo-Scottish Relations*, p. 251.
[26] Rymer, *Foedera*, vol. 1, part 2, p. 540.
[27] Stevenson (ed.), *Documents on the History of Scotland*, vol. II, p. 164.
[28] Note, for example, that it was recognized that different customs on the division of land prevailed between Irishmen and Englishmen, or that 'the killing of Englishmen and Irishmen requires different modes of punishment': *Rotuli litterarum clausarum 1204–27* (2 vols., London 1837) vol. I, p. 532; Berry (ed.), *Statutes and Ordinances of Ireland* (as cited above, ch. 1, n. 45), pp. 210–11.

common sense of nationhood, of belonging to a single 'community of the realm', emerged which in general triumphed over the fissures and contrasts in Scottish society.[29]

UNIFYING

In Wales and Ireland, on the other hand, the categorization of peoples became sharper and palpably more discriminating as the thirteenth century progressed. The Pope himself was moved to write to the king of England in 1256 to deplore the attitude of English magnates in Ireland towards the native Irish and to plead that English and Irish should be judged by the same law, 'since nature has made them equal'.[30] Such papal exhortation seems to have done little, in fact, to halt the development of discriminatory attitudes. Thus, whereas all native Irish freeholders may originally have enjoyed, or have been meant to enjoy, the protection of the criminal law under the new English dispensation in Ireland, by the mid-thirteenth century the exclusion of the free Gaelic Irish from legal rights under common law – 'exception of Irishry' as it was known – had come to prevail.[31] Attempts to rectify this discrimination in the 1270s foundered, probably on the opposition of English lords and communities in Ireland.[32] The history of official views of marriages between natives and settlers in both Wales and Ireland reflects a similar hardening of attitudes. Such marriages were common in the twelfth century and evoked no comment; as the thirteenth and fourteenth centuries progressed settlers felt the need, and indeed were statutorily required in Ireland, to seek a special licence before contracting such a mixed marriage.[33] The shift in assumptions emerges in tell-tale qualifying clauses – 'notwithstanding that she is Welsh'; 'although they are Irish'.[34] Doubtless the gap between theory and reality was massive; but the shift in assumptions hardly admits of doubt. It is paralleled in other colonial societies: thus the attitude of the British towards intermarriage with native women in India changed from an easy-going acceptance in the eighteenth century to clear disapproval later.[35] The shift in assumptions is manifested again in the creation of ethnic stereotypes and, what is more sinister, in the ensconcing of those stereotypes – be they of the treacherous

29 Barrow, *Kingship and Unity*, pp. 126–9, 153, 169; A. Grant, 'Scotland's "Celtic Fringe" in the Late Middle Ages: The MacDonald Lords of the Isles and the Kingdom of Scotland', in Davies (ed.), *The British Isles 1100–1500*, pp. 118–19.

30 Sayles (ed.), *Affairs of Ireland before the King's Council* (as cited above, ch. 1, n. 2), p. 3.

31 Brand, 'Ireland and the Literature of the Early Common Law', (as cited above ch. 4, n. 39) 96 n. 9; Nicholls, 'Anglo-French Ireland and After', 374–7. For the operation of a virtual rule of 'exception of Welshry', see Davies, *Lordship and Society in the March of Wales*, pp. 316, n. 52, 326.

32 A. J. Otway-Ruthven, 'The Request of the Irish for English Law', *Irish Historical Studies*, 6 (1948–9), pp. 261–70; A. Gwynn, 'Edward I and the proposed Purchase of English Law for the Irish, *c.* 1276–80', *Transactions Royal Historical Society*, 5th ser., 10 (1960), pp. 111–27.

33 Sayles (ed.), *Affairs of Ireland before the Kings Council*, p. 189; Berry (ed.), *Statutes and Ordinances of Ireland*, pp. 387, 412, 433.

34 *Patent Rolls of the reign of Henry III* (2 vols. London, 1901–3), 1225–32 p. 306; *Close Rolls 1251–3*, pp. 458–9.

35 Mason, *Patterns of Dominance*, p. 95.

Welsh or the fickle Irish (the labels are interchangeable) – in official thinking. The use made of such images may occasionally appear as no more than precautionary or even patronizing: 'as you well know', wrote an English official to the royal treasurer in 1296, 'Welshmen are Welshmen, and you will need to understand them properly'.[36] But there was more than a 'boys will be boys' aspect to such stereotypes. When official documents began to refer to 'the wild Irish, our enemies' or instructed that Welshmen – 'men of poor reputation' – be removed from the plains to the mountains to improve security,[37] or diagnosed the condition of those settlers who had adopted Irish habits as 'degeneracy' – in the sense of having defected from their natural affiliation to their own people (*gens*) – it is clear that images had created their own reality.[38] Hatred and suspicion became part of the reflex responses of the settler community: 'Since the Irish people (*lingua*) is hostile to you and yours', so commented the mayor and community of Cork in a petition to Edward I *c.* 1280, as if they were propounding a self-evident truth.[39] Nor was the shift in attitude confined to the settlers or to English officials; it is mirrored in a similar shift in attitudes within native society. In Wales in the thirteenth century there emerges an altogether new venom directed at the English (as they are now invariably called) as a 'foreign, alien-tongued people' who 'trample unrighteously' on the 'liberty' of the Welsh.[40] In Ireland the famous Remonstrance of *c.* 1317, addressed to the Pope in the name of Domnall Ó Néill and other Irish kings, made the point with succinct eloquence: the English settlers in Ireland 'are so dissimilar in way of life and speech . . . that there is no hope whatever of our having peace with them'.[41]

There is no single chronology to this shift in attitudes; but the early or mid-thirteenth century would appear to be an important watershed. The comment made *c.* 1205 by an English settler that 'there is a law, brought in by the English, to the effect that a donation made by an Irishman to a religious house is of no effect when the king has granted the same to an Englishman' is an early straw in the wind.[42] The chilling command of January 1217 that no Irishman was to be elected or promoted in any cathedral church in Ireland (though it was to be roundly condemned by the Pope in 1220) was another straw in the wind; the famous 'conspiracy of Mellifont' of the years 1216–31 yet another.[43] In Wales the expeditions of King John in 1211 and 1212 – the

---

[36] J. G. Edwards, 'Edward I's Castle-Building in Wales', *Proceedings of the British Academy*, 32 (1946), 80–1.

[37] H. Nicholas, *Proceedings and ordinances of the Privy Council of England* (7 vols., London, 1834–7), vol. I, p. 134; *Calendar of Chancery Warrants 1244–1326* (London, 1912), p. 448.

[38] *NHI*, vol. II, p. 310.

[39] Sayles (ed.), *Affairs of Ireland before the King's Council*, pp. 27–8.

[40] J. Morris-Jones and T. H. Parry-Williams (eds.), *Llawysgrif Hendregadredd* (Cardiff, 1933), p. 218; *Brut*, p. 110.

[41] Curtis and McDowell (eds.), *Irish Historical Documents 1172–1922*, p. 44.

[42] *Calendar of Papal Letters.*, vol. I, p. 22.

[43] *Patent Rolls 1216–25*, pp. 22–23; Watt, *The Church and the Two Nations*, pp. 85–108.

first royal expeditions to Wales for almost fifty years – seem to have accelerated the tempo of confrontation, as later did the traumatic impact of royal pressure in the years 1240–56.

Henceforth the existence of two separate peoples was institutionalized, as it were, in the governance of Wales and Ireland; assimilation was thereby made more difficult. Many of the lordships of Wales were divided into Welshries and Englishries, or Welsh counties and English counties. In Ireland there was a similar division in effect in many areas between English districts and Irishries; and, as it became evident that the conquest was to remain incomplete, an even more fundamental distinction was drawn between 'the land of peace' and 'the land of war'.[44] Attitudes became entrenched; 'since the conquest', so commented an Irish petition of the 1350s, 'there have been two kinds of people in Ireland and there still are, the English and the Irish'.[45] Administrative and legal categories rarely corresponded, of course, with social realities; they were overtaken on the ground by compromises and adjustments which made a nonsense of their neatness and clarity. They were, however, none the less real for all that. They had, or could have, practical and far-reaching consequences in matters such as jurisdiction, law, administration, land tenure, obligations and liberties; in short, in the whole fabric of social life and governance.[46] To overlook them is to ignore an essential element in the psychology and ideology of domination.

That becomes clearer when one recalls that the distinction between natives and settlers was a distinction into which discrimination was increasingly built. The Welsh and Irish were not only different; they were for many purposes inferior. That is why to call a man an Irishman when he was not was a defamatory statement actionable at law.[47] As the late thirteenth and four-teenth centuries progressed Welshmen and Irishmen became subject in theory to a host of miscellaneous exclusions on the ground of 'blood and nation'. They were – or came to be – debarred from holding certain offices, from becoming burgesses of English towns in Wales and Ireland, from the right to trade freely, or to inherit land held by English tenure, or to devise land by English law, and so forth. Such exclusions were matched by the privileges which the English communities in Wales and Ireland enjoyed and which they often flaunted. Such privileges and exclusions were often no doubt ignored in practice; but they could be, and were, activated whenever convenience dic-

---

[44] *NHI*, vol. II, p. 240.
[45] Quoted in G. J. Hand, 'English Law in Ireland, 1172–1351', *Northern Ireland Legal Quarterly*, 23 (1972), 413. For an alternative dating, Frame, *English Lordship in Ireland*, p. 4, n. 12.
[46] For an elaboration of this theme for Wales, Davies, *Lordship and Society*, pp. 302–18.
[47] G. J. Hand, *English Law in Ireland 1290–1324* (Cambridge, 1967), p. 188; J. Lydon, 'The Middle Nation', in Lydon (ed.), *The English in Medieval Ireland*, (as cited above, ch. 1, n. 46), p. 22.

tated. They naturally begat a deep sense of alienation and victimization in the native mind. So it was that a cultured fourteenth-century Welsh squire spoke poignantly of the 'pain and deprivation and exile' which he and his like suffered 'in their native land', just as an Irish court historian commented bitterly on the inversion of values in a world which classified 'the Gael' as 'ignoble though he was a landholder' while deeming the Saxon 'noble' though he lacked breeding and wealth.[48] For these men conquest was clearly much more than a military take-over; it had led, sooner or later, to the establishment of a regime in which the line between vanquished and victor was that between discrimination and privilege. It was apparently in the last decade of the thirteenth century and during the fourteenth century – at the very period when the conquest of Wales had only recently been completed and still seemed fragile and when the momentum of the English advance in Ireland was clearly faltering – that this discriminatory attitude seems to ensconce itself in the English official mind.[49] It was the mentality of men who regarded themselves as both so superior *and* so insecure that their status must be defended by privilege.

Conquering élites are not only anxious to entrench their position through privilege; they are also not infrequently imbued with a desire to shape the world they have conquered in their own image and to compel it to fall into line with their own standards. In short the cult of uniformity establishes itself. What is particularly interesting in Wales and Ireland, so it seems to me, is that it is possible to detect a gradual shift among the conquerors, and especially in the ranks of the English government, from a relatively easy-going tolerance of other people's norms to a growing insistence on the desirability of uniformity. Two quotations may serve to highlight the contrast implied in this shift. The first is an observation attributed to King Stephen of Hungary (d. 1038) that a kingdom of one language and one way of life would be weak and fragile. For King Stephen a plurality of peoples and customs within a single kingdom was a source of strength, not of weakness. It was a point of view shared by those early Anglo-Norman lords of Ireland, such as Miles de Cogan, who addressed their letters ecumenically to all the peoples under their rule, be they French, English, Irish or Welsh. The sixteenth-century Irish commentator, Richard Stanyhurst, took up a diametrically opposed position: 'Where the country is subdued, there the inhabitants ought to be ruled by the same law that the conqueror is governed by, to show the same fashion of attire wherewith the victor is vested, and to speak the same lan-

---

[48] Quoted, respectively, in Davies, *Conquest*, p. 435 and Frame, *Colonial Ireland*, p. 109.
[49] In Wales the ordinances that Edward I seems to have issued in the wake of the great revolt of 1294–5 are an early expression of this attitude, while in Ireland the legislation issued in 1297 is beginning to be imbued with the same spirit: H. Ellis (ed.), *Record of Caernarvon* (London, 1835), pp. 131–2; Berry (ed.), *Statutes and Ordinances of Ireland*, pp. 194–213.

guage that the vanquisher parleth. And if any of these three lack, doubtless the conquest limpeth'.[50]

The distance between the opinions of King Stephen and Richard Stanyhurst is not merely a function of the almost six centuries which separate them. Glimpses of the mentality of uniformity can be detected at an early date, especially – and not surprisingly – in the observations of clerics, notably with regard to ecclesiastical practices and moral standards.[51] But references to the virtues of uniformity grow apace in the later middle ages, are increasingly secular in their provenance and relate to the conduct of human affairs in general. 'It seems to us', remarked the cities of Ireland sanctimoniously, 'that where there is a diversity of law, the people cannot be of one law or of one community.' It was a viewpoint faithfully echoed in the resonant phrases of the Statute of Kilkenny (1366): 'Diversity of government and divers laws in one land cause diversity of allegiance and disputes.'[52] Once the steam-roller of uniformity was on the road nothing was to be allowed to stand in its way. So it was that the Irish should be taught the English language, since 'experience teaches us' that 'diversity of tongues' caused 'wars and divers tribulations'.[53] As for Wales, Henry VIII proclaimed his intention in 1536 to 'reduce' the Welsh 'to the perfect order, notice and knowledge of the laws of this his Realm [England] and utterly to extirpate all and singular the sinister usages and customs differing from the same'.[54]

The reasons for this growing emphasis on the benefits and indeed the necessity of uniformity, especially in official governmental circles, are doubtless manifold. We might locate some of them in those profound changes which overtook European society in the twelfth and thirteenth centuries as an international church developed its theological, ecclesiastical and moral codes and elaborated a machinery for imposing those codes across the continent; as cathedral schools and universities fostered a common curriculum of knowledge and accepted forms of intellectual argument; as lay governance became more confident of its capacity, and indeed its responsibility, to order the affairs of society; and as a broad consensus appeared among those who considered themselves educated and civilized as to the norms of social behaviour, manners, governance and economic activity. Europe was in the grip of its own self-confidence, especially towards those whom it regarded as on the margins of its own society (such as the Welsh and the Irish) or outside it (such as Moslems and Jews). It was also in the grip of its own rationality. Men of

---

50 Quoted, respectively, in Reynolds, *Kingdoms and Communities*, p. 257 and J. F. Lydon, *The Lordship of Ireland in the Middle Ages* (London, 1972), p. 281.

51 See, for example, *Expugnatio*, pp. 98–101 (Bk 1. ch. 35), 142–3 (Bk 2, ch. 5); Ralph of Diceto, *Opera Historica*, vol. 1, p. 350; Watt, *The Church and the Two Nations*, p. 132.

52 Hand, 'English Law in Ireland, 1172–1351', 413; Curtis and McDowell, *Irish Historical Documents 1172–1922*, p. 53.

53 E. Perroy, *L'Angleterre et le grand schisme d'occident* (Paris, 1933), pp. 395, 403.

54 W. Rees, *The Union of England and Wales* (Cardiff, 1948), p. 55 (27 Henry VIII, ch. 26).

reason have always been impatient of deviations from the self-evident truth of their own abstract nouns. That, for example, was the ultimate condemnation of Welsh law: it deviated from 'right' (*jus*), 'from the line of justice' (*a justicie linea*), 'from justice and reason'.[55] The men of the age of the *summa* had little time for local customs, especially barbaric customs.

The cult of uniformity was also surely promoted, albeit unconsciously, by the growing use of the written word as the vehicle of government command. Where power is based on oral command, where law is essentially localized and customary (and considered none the worse for that), where the flexibility and convenient amnesia of present memory is the basis of precedent, there the ideology of uniformity has limited scope to develop. But where there are manuals on procedure to be consulted and legal treatises and registers of writs to be dispatched; where collections of native law can be allegedly examined (as happened in Ireland, Wales and Scotland in turn) and found wanting by the canons of jurisprudence and the practices of English law; where historical precedents from records, especially those of the English government, can be assembled to prove a claim (as happened in the pursuit of English domination in both Wales and Scotland in the late thirteenth century) a new mentality begins to prevail.[56] It is the mentality where truth and right are determined by the written record, more specifically the written record of the victors.

The creators, and keepers, of the written record were the bureaucrats. Bureaucrats have ever been the advocates of uniformity; indeed without uniformity their world is shattered, their authority undermined. How far the growth of bureaucratic attitudes contributed to the growth of a mentality of uniformity and a changed perception of the governance of conquered lands can be briefly indicated by contrasting the Anglo-Norman impact on Wales and Ireland.[57] The conquest of Wales began in what may be called the pre-bureaucratic age. It was an unco-ordinated, piecemeal, aristocratic-dominated movement. It made no attempt to introduce a uniform or centralized pattern of governance into the conquered lands; on the contrary, its legacy was a collection of large lordships, notable for the diversity of their customs and for their almost total independence from the normal governmental and judicial machinery of the English kingdom. The March of Wales, as this area was known, even sported – and was allowed to sport – its own law or rather laws, a hybrid collection of local customs and compromises known as 'the law of the March'.[58] The contrast with the English penetration of Ireland could not be

[55] Quoted in Davies, 'Law and National Identity', 66.

[56] See in general J. Goody (ed.), *Literacy in Traditional Society* (Cambridge, 1968), pp. 55–68; M. T. Clanchy, 'Literacy, Law and the Power of the State', *Culture et idéologie dans la gènese de l'état moderne* (Rome, 1985), pp. 25–34.

[57] See also, though from a different angle, A. J. Otway-Ruthven, 'The Constitutional Position of the Great Lordships of South Wales', *Transactions Royal Historical Society*, 5th series, 8 (1958), pp. 1–20.

[58] R. R. Davies, 'The Law of the March', *Welsh History Review*, 5 (1970–1) 1–30.

sharper. Similarities, of course, there are in abundance – notably in the aristocratic and piecemeal character of the conquest, the emergence of powerful local supremacies and the varieties of compromises with native customs and society. But the two conquests are fundamentally distinguished in their character by the growth, in the formative period of almost a century which separates them, of bureaucratic notions of uniformity and centralized control and of the acceptance of the custom of the king's court as the common law of England. From an early stage of English royal intervention in Ireland, and increasingly so from John's reign onwards, there is a regular flow of commands insisting on the necessity of uniformity of governmental practice with the English norm – on matters such as governmental organization, law, jurisdiction, coinage, and weights and measures. Selective borrowings and hybrid local customs which characterized the law of the March in Wales were not, at least officially, to be permitted in Ireland; equally the appearance of Marcher-type liberties was nipped in the bud in Ireland by the reservation to the king of the four major pleas, by the insistence that royal writs ran within and without franchise, and by a jurisdiction in error which theoretically allowed cases to be taken on appeal from a liberty court to a royal court.[59] 'The king wills . . . that all customs which are kept in the realm of England be kept in Ireland and that the said land be subject to the said laws and be ruled by them.'[60] Such an edict could admittedly apply only to those parts of Ireland under firm English rule and in which there was a substantial English settler population. Nevertheless the tone of the command epitomizes the shift in attitudes at the heart of the present argument. The tone is royalist, England-centred and uniformist. It is the language of the mid-thirteenth century; it could not have been the language of a century earlier.

The same shift is registered in the way that conquest now implies an increasing degree of administrative integration and central direction. The change in approach was most immediately apparent in Ireland, and that for obvious reasons. The institutions of English royal governance – exchequer, chancery, justiciar, writs, shires and so forth – were exported thither ready-made; likewise some of the officers – judges, exchequer officials, chancery clerks and such like – who serviced these institutions in England now found themselves dispatched on a tour of duty to man similar institutions in Ireland. The administrative transplant was, it is true, effected rather slowly and in a piecemeal fashion, and the limits of its practical success soon became evident. Yet the significance of the enterprise is surely not open to doubt: for the first time the institutions of English governance had been transported *en bloc* to a conquered country. Such an imposition of royal administration was not so easily achieved in Wales, since aristocratic rulers had been allowed a free hand there to shape their own supremacies and institutions. But with the

[59] Otway-Ruthven, *Ireland*, ch. 5 remains the best introduction.
[60] *Calendar of Patent Rolls 1232–47*, p. 488.

dramatic increase in the direct royal presence in the country in the 1240s, English institutions were quickly introduced into the crown lands in north-east and south-west Wales; and when Edward I finally conquered Gwynedd in 1283 he quickly carved it into shires and hundreds, created the new offices of sheriff and coroner and established at Caernarfon a replica version in miniature of the royal administration at Westminster (and Dublin). There was no need, of course, for a similar transplant of English institutions into Scotland in 1296 when Edward I, in the words of a contemporary diarist, 'conquered and serched the kingdom'. But a junta of English officers was introduced to run the governance of the kingdom; an exchequer was established at Berwick which was to be precisely modelled on its Westminster prototype; and two escheators were appointed, in line with English practice, to guard the Crown's feudal revenues.[61]

The degree of governmental uniformity and integration that the king's lands in the British Isles enjoyed by 1300 was very far indeed from being complete and was much less complete and effective in practice than bureaucratic theory and aspiration suggested. Yet it was far greater in intention and achievement than could have been imagined a century or so earlier. Accounts from the exchequers at Dublin, Berwick, Caernarfon and Carmarthen were audited at Westminster; cases were sent there on appeal to the court of the king's bench; petitions from Ireland, Wales and Scotland were laid before the king's council and in parliament; English statutes and proclamations were dispatched, where appropriate, for placarding in Wales, Ireland and even Scotland.[62] 'As it is done in England', *come est fait en Angleterre*, was the recurrent refrain of this mentality of administrative unity. A metropolitan view of authority and of the norms of governance was extending outwards to embrace all the king's lands in the British Isles.

Administrative unity opened the route to the political integration of those lands; in other words it opened up the prospect of a truly united kingdom. Others had already long since dreamt such dreams. Churchmen, as so often, were among the most zealous visionaries. 'It was expedient for the union and solidarity of the kingdom', so Archbishop Lanfranc of Canterbury had argued in the eleventh century, 'that all Britain should be subject to one primate.'[63] Lanfranc's ideal of a pan-British kingdom and church was not necessarily shared by his political masters. Indeed neither the Norman nor the Angevin kings regarded the various dominions they ruled as necessarily, or even desireably, a unit other than in dynastic terms. They could add to them as opportunity arose, but equally they could subtract from them as family needs

61 Stevenson (ed.), *Documents on the History of Scotland*, vol. II, pp. 31, 163–4; Barrow, *Bruce*, pp. 75–6; Prestwich, *Edward I*, p. 474.
62 Cf. F. M. Powicke, *The Thirteenth Century 1216–1307* (Oxford, 1953), pp. 711–12.
63 Hugh the Chanter, *History of the Church of York, 1066–1277*, ed. C. Johnson (London, 1961), pp. 2–3.

dictated. Thus Ireland might well have been hived off to a cadet branch of the royal family, as was clearly intended in 1177. Even as late as John's reign, occasional references to a 'kingdom of Ireland' alongside the 'kingdom of England' may suggest that the mentality of aggregation and dismemberment was not altogether dead.[64]

A generation or so later it was dead and buried, at least in official circles. When in 1254 the lord Edward was given an endowment which included all the royal territories in Wales and the lordship of Ireland it was specifically decreed that those lands were 'never (to) be separated from the Crown, but should remain entirely to the kings of England for ever'.[65] A concept of an inalienable royal fisc had emerged and was extended to include the Crown's lordships and estates in Ireland and Wales. An associated viewpoint, albeit from a different perspective, had already informed a letter of 1246 imposing the laws of England on Ireland 'for the common benefit of the land of Ireland and for the unity of the king's lands'.[66] The letter's reference to 'the common good' shows how far the explanatory language of monarchical action was changing in the thirteenth century; but it is the allusion to 'the unity of the king's lands' which is above all significant for the present argument. Once 'unity' is regarded as the norm and the governance of conquered lands is embraced within that 'unity' then the nature of domination over conquered peoples will surely begin to change. Political integration, not aggregation, is now the goal.

There was more than one road to unity. One was to integrate the outlying dependencies more firmly into the body of the realm of England through a combination of feudal and jurisdictional pressure and political power, in other words through the intensification of overlordship. Wales in the 1240s and again in the 1270s and Scotland in the 1290s were candidates for such treatment. Ideally such integration could have been achieved peacefully; tactful pressure should have been sufficient. Thus during the course of his first campaign against Gwynedd in 1277, Edward I struck a bargain with the two Welsh claimants whom he backed against Llywelyn ap Gruffudd. One of the conditions of the bargain was that they were 'to come to our parliaments in England as our other earls and barons come'.[67] John Balliol was expected to toe the same line after his election as king of Scotland in 1292. 'He came to our parliaments at our command', remarked Edward I magisterially of him, 'and was present in them *as our subject, like others of our realm*.'[68] It was not altogether fanciful for a sixteenth-century reconstruction of an Edwardian parliament to seat Llywelyn of Wales and Alexander III of Scotland on either side of Edward I.[69] Edward I meant to be master of all the British Isles and

---

[64] Rymer, *Foedera*, vol. I, part 1, p. 111.   [65] Rymer, *Foedera*, vol. I, part 2, p. 297.
[66] *Calendar of Patent Rolls 1232–47*, p. 488; *Foedera*, vol. I, part 1, p. 266. It is noteworthy that Edward was not called lord of Ireland during his father's lifetime, *NHI*, vol. II, p. 179.
[67] *Litt. Wallie*, p. 104   [68] Stones (ed.), *Anglo-Scottish Relations*, pp. 210–11 (my italics).
[69] This pictorial reconstruction has been reproduced many times, most recently in Prestwich, *Edward I*, p. 14

wanted his mastery acknowledged by Welsh prince and Scottish king by attendance in his parliament.

The Welsh and the Scots denied him such a mastery by peaceful means. Instead Edward I had to resort to confiscation and conquest to attain his ends. The terms in which the confiscation was justified reveal a good deal about the mentality of mastery in the late-thirteenth century. References to ecclesiastical permission and spiritual reform – though not altogether absent, especially in Wales – do not figure as prominently as they had in Ireland in the twelfth century; nor is there that primal exultation in prowess and plunder so characteristic of the *chansons de gestes*. Instead, the apologetics of conquest have become secular and legalistic, and the urge for domination was expressed in terms of feudal dependence, jurisdictional control, good governance and political mastery. There is a new chilling tone in the language of the conqueror: 'to put an end finally to … the malice of the Welsh', as Edward I remarked impatiently in 1282, or 'to make an end of the business', as he commented menacingly on the Scottish problem in 1306.[70] The language of the relationship was feudal; but in both Wales and Scotland no one could have been under any illusion that the struggle was ultimately one about power and domination, the domination of Britain.

How the mood had changed from earlier times we can notice again in the insistence on the total submission of the conquered peoples. Abject surrender was now the order of the day. In July 1283, on the morrow of defeat, a series of regional assemblies in Wales bound themselves over in large sums to abide by the peace that Edward I had imposed on the country;[71] and in the preamble of the Statute of Wales in the following year the king could proudly declare that the inhabitants of Wales had submitted themselves utterly (*alto et basse*) to his will. This was the conquest of a people, not just the defeat of its prince. Likewise just over a dozen years later Edward's triumph in Scotland was marked by the exaction of oaths of fealty from all substantial freeholders in the country, so that, in Professor Barrow's words, 'in future his subjects in North Britain should be on precisely the same footing as his subjects south of the Border'.[72] Thorough was at work; the rituals of 'a full and complete conquest' were being celebrated.

Such a conquest entailed the eradication of the memory of the conquered peoples. Wales was given the treatment in 1283–4: its most treasured royal insignia (including the prince's coronet and the jewel or crown of King Arthur) were removed; while its most famous relic, a fragment of the True Cross (*Y Groes Naid*), was paraded in a great triumphal procession through London and later accompanied Edward I, appropriately enough, on his invasion of Scotland. The conqueror was appropriating the past of the conquered people in order to replace it by his own emblems of victory. Scotland's turn came, of

---

[70] *Calendar of Various Chancery Rolls*, p. 275; Powicke, *The Thirteenth Century*, p. 706.
[71] *Litt. Wallie*, pp. 151, 154–7.   [72] Barrow, *Bruce*, p. 76.

course, in 1296: jewelry, relics, plate and regalia were removed; and the Stone of Destiny was transported to England, 'as a sign of the resignation and conquest of the kingdom' as Walter of Guisborough put it.[73] That many of these Welsh and Scottish relics were now deposited in Westminster abbey, the religious headquarters of the English monarchy, and were indeed physically fastened onto the shrine of Edward the Confessor,[74] the proprietal saint of that monarchy, made it clear that the conquest now entailed a conscious campaign for the obliteration of the native past and the creation of a new ideology of victorious unity. It was in the pursuit of that same ambition that Archbishop Pecham ordered the clergy to undertake a campaign for the political re-education of the Welsh after the conquest, in order to wean them from their Trojan fantasies and from their messianic hopes of recovering the mastery of the whole of Britain.[75] The conqueror was no longer content with domination; he now also wanted to win the hearts and minds of men to his way of thinking.

And also to his way of ruling. A united kingdom was in the making; it is a far cry from the 'ramshackle family consortium', as the Angevin lands of the late twelfth century have been memorably called. The language is now that of assimilation as much as that of addition and annexation. The title 'prince of Wales' was not added to the royal style after 1283, nor that of 'king of Scotland' after 1296.[76] There was no need, or room, for more than one king in the new Britain; the royal style was the same in Scotland and Wales as it was in England. Wales, so Edward I declared grandly in 1284, 'hitherto subject to us by feudal right has now been wholly and entirely transferred under our direct rule (*in proprietatis nostre dominium*) ... and (has been) annexed and united ... unto the Crown of the aforesaid Realm (of England) as a member of the said body'. Edward I did not use such incorporative language in the case of Scotland but there also he proclaimed his 'right of full dominion' and his 'full right, by reason of property and possession'.[77] In both Wales and Scotland the consequence of conquest was spelt out pointedly by referring to both countries as lands (*terre*) rather than as a principality or a kingdom.

The days of a single kingdom of the British Isles may not have arrived. But the nature of the dominion exercised by Edward I within his lands in Britain was very different in aim and ambition from that claimed and exercised by Henry I or even Henry II. The concentration of ultimate political and governmental power at Westminster seemed to inaugurate, however tentatively, the prospect of a single, united, England-centred kingdom. Neither

[73] H. Rothwell (ed.), *The Chronicle of Walter of Guisborough*, Camden Series, vol. LXXXIX (London, 1957), p. 281.

[74] Stevenson (ed.), *Documents on the History of Scotland*, vol. II, p. 135.

[75] C. T. Martin (ed.), *Registrum Epistolarum fratris Johannis Peckham*, Rolls Series (3 vols. London, 1882–5), vol. II, pp. 741–2.

[76] M. Prestwich, 'Colonial Scotland: The English in Scotland under Edward I', in R. A. Mason (ed.), *Scotland and England 1286–1815* (Edinburgh, 1987), pp. 6–7.

[77] Stones (ed.), *Anglo-Scottish Relations*, pp. 216–17.

Wales nor Ireland nor Scotland was, of course, absorbed into England, nor was there the prospect that such absorption could be quickly effected. But the stamp of the king of England's ultimate authority now lay over his lands throughout the British Isles. It demonstrated itself visually, as in the great hall built at Dublin castle in the 1240s after the model of the hall of the archbishop of Canterbury and decorated with a painting of the king and queen with their baronage, or in the deliberately imperial majesty of Caernarfon castle, with its evocation of the walls of Constantinople and its statue of the king above the great twin-towered gatehouse. It demonstrated itself authoritatively, as in the command that 'all his subjects are bound by their allegiances to obey his orders under the great seal of England', whether they lived in Scotland, Ireland, Wales or England itself.[78]

The tide of English power over the British Isles appeared to reach its height in 1305.[79] In the Lenten parliament that year long lists of petitions from Ireland, Scotland and Gascony were considered by Edward I's councillors, while an equally impressive batch of petitions from north and west Wales was being simultaneously scrutinized by Prince Edward's council at Kennington. The arm of the king of England's justice seemed to reach to the farthest parts of the British Isles – be it Anglesey in Wales, Kerry in Ireland or Galloway in Scotland. In a second parliament in September 1305 ten representatives chosen on behalf of the community of Scotland spent three weeks at Westminster discussing with the king's councillors an Ordinance for the government of the land of Scotland. Wales had been conquered; Scotland had at last submitted; Ireland was a lordship held by the king of England. Contemporaries were aware that a single kingship of the British Isles was on the cards. It appeared so even in distant Connacht. 'Edward the Great, king of England, Wales and Scotland, duke of Gascony and lord of Ireland, rested in Christ', so recorded the annalist in 1307. 'The crown of the king of England, Wales, Ireland and Scotland', he added, 'was afterwards given to Edward, son of Edward.'[80] Peter Langtoft, the rhyming canon of Bridlington, was naturally more eloquent and unrestrained in saluting Edward's achievement:

Now are the islanders all joined together,
And Albany reunited to the regalities
Of which King Edward is proclaimed lord.
Cornwall and Wales are in his power
And Ireland the great at his will.
There is neither king nor prince of all the countries
Except King Edward, who thus has united them.[81]

[78] *Calendar of Close Rolls 1339–41*, p. 259; *Calendar of Close Rolls 1288–96*, p. 200
[79] For this theme see R. R. Davies, 'In Praise of British History' in Davies (ed.), *The British Isles 1110–1500*, pp. 22–3.
[80] *Annals of Connacht*, p. 213.
[81] T. Wright (ed.), *The Chronicle of Pierre de Langtoft*, Rolls Series (2 vols., London, 1866–8), vol. II, pp. 264–7.

Whether King Edward had or had not achieved as much would remain to be seen; but Peter's poetic effusion is there to remind us that concepts of domination had given way to an ideology of unity, uniformity and conquest. That, surely, was one of the more momentous changes to have overtaken the British Isles in the twelfth and thirteenth centuries.

Index

WITHDRAWN